The History of Lincolnville, South Carolina

Christine W. Hampton
Rosalee W. Washington

2007

The History of Lincolnville, South Carolina

Christine W. Hampton
Rosalee W. Washington

Copyright © 2007 Christine W. Hampton and Rosalee W. Washington
All rights reserved.
ISBN: 978-1-419-66323-9
Library of Congress Control Number: 2007901861

To order additional copies, please contact us.
BookSurge, LLC
www.booksurge.com
1-866-308-6235
orders@booksurge.com

Edited by Stephen G. Hoffius
Book Design by Anja U. Kelley

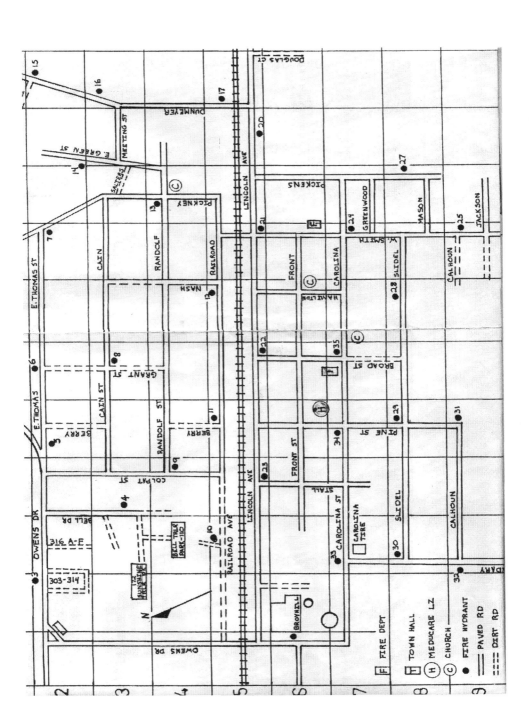

Dedication

This book is dedicated with love in memory of our father, Christopher Elijah Williams, and in honor of our mother, Anna Rebecca Williams.

We also dedicate this book to our husbands, James C. Hampton and Arnic J. Washington, who lovingly supported us during the entire process of this project.

Contents

Acknowledgments	vii
The Founding of Lincolnville	1
Abraham Lincoln	5
Richard Harvey Cain	7
Lincolnville Mayors	11
The Great Lincolnville Earthquake	37
Lincolnville Elementary School	39
Lincolnville Churches	53
Ebenezer African Methodist Episcopal Church	53
Ebenezer A.M.E. Sunday School	63
Wesley Methodist Episcopal Church	70
Mount Zion Baptist Church	73
Nazareth Holiness Church of Deliverance #2	76
Friendship Inspirational Church of God in Christ	78
Lydia Baptist Church	80
Lincolnville Police Department	81
Lincolnville Volunteer Fire Department	87
Civic League	93
Highlighting Citizens	99
Wilhemenia Alston Barron	99
James Christopher Hampton	101
David Seabrook Hill	103
Alonzo William Holman	104
Dr. Lawrence James	107
John Henry McCray	109
Richard A. Ready	111
Charlotte S. Riley	113
Pernessa C. Seele	117
Stephen Towns	119
Military	121
Glimpses of the Past	133
A Look into the Future	161
"Oh Lincolnville" by Frank Dunn	163
About the Authors	165
Photo Credits	169
Index	171

Acknowledgments

During the course of researching and writing the history of Lincolnville many individuals and groups generously assisted us in collecting information and preparing this book. Therefore we would like to extend our sincere thanks to all who supported us in this endeavor:

Groups:
Avery Research Center (College of Charleston), Berkeley County Health Department, Berkeley County Library (Moncks Corner and Goose Creek), Charleston County Courthouse, Charleston County Public Library (Main Branch, Dart Branch, and Bookmobile), Charleston County School District Archives, Charleston Library Society, Coastal Community Foundation, Ebenezer A.M.E. Church, Emanuel A.M.E. Church, Lincolnville Comprehensive Planning Guide, Lincolnville Town Records, Lowcountry Quarterly Grants Program, the National Archives and Records Administration (Washington, D.C.), National Trust for Historic Preservation (Charleston office), South Carolina Department of Archives and History, South Caroliniana Library (University of South Carolina)

Individuals:
Bernice Aiken, Mayor Tyrone Aiken, Helen Anderson, Naomi Bacote, Gail Bunkum, Rev. Hayward Cordes, Sr., Attorney Ruth W. Cupp, Frank Dunn, Attorney Bernard Fielding, Michael German, Rev. Anna Ruth Williams Gleaton, Dorothy Glover, Rochelle A. Greene, James C. Hampton, Louise Hill, Rev. Alonzo W. Holman, Gerald Holman, Carolyn A. Howard, George Jacobs, Sr., Bishop J.J. Jennings, Jr., Alma Latten, Dr. Crystal Lucky, Clayton Mance, Jr.,

Emily Manley Nelson, Lucille Noble, Lewis Ruffin Noisette, Helene S. Polk, Dr. Bernard Powers, Rev. Leon Salley, Pernessa C. Seele, Carrie L. Sellers, Carolee Simmons, Pearly M. Smalls, Stephen Towns, Arnic J. Washington, Mildred Mance Wigfall, Rev. Anna Rebecca Williams, Clayton Williams, Geraldine D. Williams, Jessie Williams, and Gwendolyn Wright.

Finally, we thank our editor, Stephen Hoffius, who patiently advised and guided us through our first endeavor in recording the history of the Town of Lincolnville. By working with him, we have gained much information, experience, and skills to bring this project to a successful completion.

Literary Sources:
Elias B. Bull research files, South Carolina Room, Charleston County Public Library
Charleston Chronicle
Charleston Post and Courier
Maurine Christopher, *America's Black Congressmen* (New York: Crowell, 1971)
Rev. Mrs. Charlotte S. Riley, *A Mysterious Life and Calling* (Charleston, S.C.: Industrial Department, Jenkins Orphanage, n.d.) (copy at Wilberforce University)
Annie Mae Harris et al, comps., Berkeley Training High School 50th Class Reunion booklet
Luella Seele, "A Study of Lincolnville, S.C.: A Negro Communnity" (Master's thesis, School of Education, Atlanta University, 1956)
Danny Smith, *The Negro in Congress: 1870-1901* (Port Washington, N.Y.: Kennikat Press, 1966)
Carter G. Woodson, *The Negro in Our History* (Washington, D.C.: Associated Publishers, 1931)
www.lincolnvillesc.com

Technical Support:
Sarah Bozier, James C. Hampton, Stephen Hoffius, Olivia Horlback, Anja U. Kelley, Carolyn Venner

The History of Lincolnville, South Carolina

Christine W. Hampton
Rosalee W. Washington

The Founding of Lincolnville

In South Carolina in the first decade after the end of the Civil War, African Americans were freed, but they weren't yet free. In every issue they addressed — politics, education, health care, law enforcement — they met resistance from whites who refused to give up the power they had always held. For a short golden moment, roughly 1865 to 1876, blacks took positions in city councils and the state legislature, schools and police forces. They had to struggle for each achievement, and in 1876 they were thrown out of power after a period of white terrorism never before seen in this country.

Many African Americans chose another route: They would handle their own affairs. They decided to establish their own cities, control all local agencies, and take care of each other.

So it was that in 1867, seven men, headed by Richard Harvey Cain, an A.M.E. minister, took a ride on the South Carolina Special, a local train. They were looking for sites that the South Carolina Railway Company wanted to sell. The land they decided to purchase became Lincolnville. (Another African-American town founded about this time — 1870 — was Promised Land in Abbeville County. Maryville, in Charleston County, was chartered in 1886 and incorporated in 1888.)

The Lincolnville town site was one mile from Summerville, in what was then Berkeley County. Through the years, Berkeley, Dorchester, and Charleston counties would all wrangle over which jurisdiction the town was located in, and today Lincolnville is in Charleston County.

The site was called Pump Pond, or Pump Swamp, or Pump Pond Swamp, because the train stopped there to take on water, wood, and later coal. It featured the highest elevation in the area.

Three swamps were found nearby, all of which still exist, all flowing to Eagle Creek and then on to the Ashley River. The western swamp was the largest, located about a mile north of Pump Pond. It became known as the Sawmill Swamp, after a local business powered by the flowing water. A gristmill was established there, too. The easternmost swamp was crossed by a brick arched culvert for the train crossing, and became known as the Brick Arch Swamp.

According to legend, the railroad workers and settlers called the area Pump Pond, but when surveyors asked local people the name they misunderstood the pronunciation. They recorded it as Pon Pon. This name and several others were used until the charter was granted in 1889. Other names were Lincoln Village, the Village of Lincoln, and, finally, Lincolnville.

The seven founders of Lincolnville, all A.M.E. church trustees, were Daniel Adger, Marc Buffett, Rev. Richard Harvey Cain, Hector Grant, Rev. Lewis Ruffin Nichols, Rev. M.B. Salters, and Walter Steele. Rev. Salters was the pastor of Morris Brown A.M.E. Church in Charleston. No doubt he was a close personal friend of Reverend Cain, a U.S. congressmen in the 1870s and one of the most dynamic black leaders of 19th-century America.

The men paid just $1,000 to the South Carolina Railway for 620 acres of land. They agreed that two-thirds of the proceeds of any land they sold would be returned to the railroad.

In 1886 charges were made that Bishop Cain had not paid for the land, and the Berkeley County sheriff tried to resell all of the land, including those lots that made up Lincolnville. The names of Lincolnville property owners who filed papers to protect their lands included Isaac Robinson and A. Tony Williams. A judge in February 1887 agreed with the Lincolnville residents and decreed that none of the town lands should be sold.

By the time the town was chartered in 1889 many lots had been sold and now held houses; a school and Ebenezer A.M.E. Church also had been established. The town's dedication to education was so strong that eventually it caused a small problem. A century after its founding, the city's boundaries were confused because three early schools had been built, and the 1889 town charter proclaimed that the town's "limits shall extend one half mile in every direction from the schoolhouse." But which schoolhouse?

The town was incorporated on December 24, 1889, by African-American attorney Samuel J. Lee of Charleston, who had defended the Lincolnville property owners in 1887. Lee was the former speaker of the S.C. House of Representatives, a trustee of the South Carolina College (now the University of South Carolina), and, according to one source, "by the 1880s the state's leading black lawyer." The charter established that the town would be governed by an intendant (later called the mayor), and four wardens. Marc Buffett, E.K. Holman, Samuel F. Peterson, and Henry Mickens were appointed the town's first Board of Managers with the responsibility to hold the first election. The settlers named the town in honor of President Abraham Lincoln, whose Emancipation Proclamation had freed enslaved people in the South.

Abraham Lincoln

Reverend Cain and the other founders of the new black town near Summerville must have found it easy to choose the name Lincolnville. After his murder in 1865, Abraham Lincoln's name was applied to a wide range of things all around the country — streets, towns, schools, companies — especially by African Americans who wanted to honor his achievements that benefited black people.

According to the *African American Encyclopedia* (second edition):

"Key policies of the [Lincoln] administration that had consequences for African American lives were two Confiscation Acts, a bill abolishing slavery in the District of Columbia, a preliminary Proclamation of Emancipation, the Emancipation Proclamation, the Conscription Act, a bill granting African Americans in the armed forces equal pay with whites, and the Thirteenth Amendment to the Constitution."

Of particular importance were the Emancipation Proclamation and the Thirteenth Amendment to the Constitution.

"On January 1, 1863, President Lincoln issued the Emancipation Proclamation, stating that slaves of the Confederacy were free. The Emancipation Proclamation did not affect slave states that had not left the union or areas in the Confederate states under Union control. For these states and areas, Lincoln encouraged willing, compensated liberation of slaves. . . .

"On January 31, 1865, Congress passed the Thirteenth Amendment to the Constitution, abolishing slavery in the United States. The amendment was ratified on December 18, 1865. The Civil War officially ended at Appomattox Courthouse in central Virginia on April 9, 1865, with the surrender of Confederate general-in-chief Robert E. Lee. Days later, on April 15, President Lincoln was assassinated."

Though President Lincoln did not live to see the results of his actions, he provided African Americans throughout the country with the opportunity to rise from slavery and become educated, self-supporting citizens. Richard Harvey Cain and the other founders of Lincolnville took the inevitable next steps when they founded a town named for the former president, where opportunities were not limited by bigotry and prejudice.

Richard Harvey Cain

Near the end of the Civil War, a man of vision arrived in Charleston, South Carolina. He was an African Methodist Episcopal Church missionary who was sent to Charleston to help reorganize Emanuel A.M.E. Church. Richard Harvey Cain wanted to continue building on ideas started by earlier A.M.E. bishops.

  Cain's life began on April 12, 1825, in Greenbrier County, Virginia. He was born a free child because his parents were free. He was the son of a Cherokee Indian mother and an African father. In 1832 he moved with his parents to Gallipolis, Ohio. There he began his formal education. As a young man he worked on a steamboat on the Ohio River but soon found that his interest lay in religious work. He was converted in 1841 to the Methodist Episcopal Church at the age of 16, but the discrimination he met there led him to join the African Methodist Episcopal Church. In 1859 he was ordained a deacon in the A.M.E. church. Cain, realizing that he needed more formal education enrolled in Wilberforce University in 1860. He was assigned as pastor of a church in Brooklyn, New York, the next year, and served as a pastor in New York from 1861 to 1865. He was then assigned to Charleston, South Carolina, to stimulate religious activity among the freedmen.

  Soon after arriving in Charleston, he began his work. Under Reverend Cain's leadership, funds were raised to purchase property on Calhoun Street to build Emanuel A.M.E. Church. The architect for that building was Robert Vesey, son of Denmark Vesey, who organized his famous conspiracy against slavery and slave owners throughout the city, especially in Charleston's A.M.E. churches.

Reverend Cain's ministerial duties in South Carolina extended to Summerville, Lincolnville, Georgetown, Marion, and Sumter. However, even with so much church responsibility, he had too much energy to be confined to these duties. He participated in whatever touched the lives of his people.

Due to the unrest and mistreatment of blacks in Charleston, Cain began purchasing land in the surrounding area. In 1867, Cain and several other men purchased land which became the town of Lincolnville. The property purchased to settle Lincolnville was divided and sold to blacks who wanted a place to be free.

Richard Harvey Cain

Not much is known about Cain's personal life, but records of land transactions show that he was married to Laura H. Cain. Richard and Laura Cain sold property to Susan Owens on August 28, 1876, on Pinckney Street in Lincolnville.

Richard Harvey Cain was deeply involved in politics in South Carolina. He served as a member of the Reconstruction Constitutional Convention in 1868 and played an important role in rebuilding the government of the state along liberal lines. There he argued that the state constitution should provide all children the benefits of a publicly funded education. As a member of the S.C. Land Commission, he argued for the redistribution of farmland. He offered a resolution asking Congress to appropriate $1 million for the purchase of land in South Carolina as a measure of relief for freedmen. Although his resolution was not accepted, the idea was incorporated in the establishment of the South Carolina Land Commission in 1869. Throughout the Reconstruction era, Cain believed that land ownership was the means by which blacks could achieve progress and prosperity.

In 1872, Rev. Richard Harvey Cain won an at-large seat in the 43rd Congress. He was the first black to win a statewide political campaign in the history of South Carolina. Cain won a second term in 1877 representing Charleston.

At various times, Cain supported the African emigration movement and printed a standing editorial in the *Missionary Record* entitled "Ho for Africa!" In support of the Liberia emigration movement of 1877-78, he sponsored a bill to pay passage for those who desired to return to Africa.

Richard Cain had strong racial feelings. During his political experiences he received the nickname of "Daddy Cain," which was used in derision by whites and in respect and admiration by Negroes. Probably his most sensational statement was the expression of his hope that the time would come, "When there would be no black, no white — but one common brotherhood and one united people, going forward in the progress of the nation." Cain claimed that mixed schools would work no harm, as South Carolina College (later named the University of South Carolina) had not suffered as a result of having a mixed student body after the Civil War. Another statement, which shows Cain's thinking: "I want to shake hands over the bloody chasm — I desire to bury the tomahawk forever."

Cain edited two Republican newspapers during Reconstruction. In 1866 he took over leadership of the *South Carolina Leader*. He was also editor of the *Missionary Record*, the official paper of the South Carolina A.M.E. conference and one of the most influential newspapers in the state.

After Reconstruction, Reverend Cain moved to Texas and was elected president of Paul Quinn College. In 1880 he was appointed bishop in the African Methodist Episcopal Church. He was unable to answer the roll call at the Quarto-centennial Conference in 1887 because he answered the call of death on January 18, 1887, in Washington, D.C. He is buried in Graceland Cemetery in Washington, D. C. Emanuel and Morris Brown A.M.E. churches in Charleston have marble memorials to this great patriarch in their main sanctuaries.

The Town of Lincolnville celebrates the life of Richard Harvey Cain by giving the Richard Harvey Cain Award to a citizen who lives or has lived in Lincolnville and has contributed to the improvement of the town of Lincolnville. This award is presented at the annual Lincolnville Heritage Festival. The first three recipients were Sonia Glover (2003), Rev. Alonzo Holman (2004), Rosalee Williams Washington (2005), and Pernessa Seele (2006).

A statement by the eminent historian Carter G. Woodson best summarizes Cain's life: "He was generally referred to even by his enemies, as an upright and honest man who deserved the good will of all citizens."

Lincolnville Mayors

Intendant Lewis Ruffin Nichols

Rev. Lewis Ruffin Nichols, the first mayor of Lincolnville, was born in December 1847 in Raleigh, North Carolina, the grandson of Robert and Hicksey Nichols. The latter was of Indian descent and therefore was born free. Their son, Robert Nichols, Jr., married Marthena Lewis and became the parent of Robert Nichols III, Louisa Nichols, Stephan Nichols, and Lewis Ruffin Nichols.

Rev. Lewis Ruffin Nichols received his early education in Raleigh, and continued his education under Harris Leland of Boston.

On February 14, 1875, Reverend Nichols, 28 years old, married Anna Elizabeth Cotton. Some of their children were: William E. Nichols, Benjamin S. Nichols, Samuel W. Nichols, Henry M. Nichols, Katie N. Kennedy, Marthena E. Cooper, Della W. Williams, Louisa Nichols, Beatrice Noisette, and Nancy Eunice Nichols.

Intendant Lewis Ruffin Nichols

Intendant Nichols and his family

Reverend Nichols gave his life to the Lord and soon after that, in 1872, began preaching in Greensboro, North Carolina. Throughout his ministry, Reverend Nichols dedicated his life to working diligently as God's messenger. During his work in the church he touched countless lives, spreading the gospel in many localities in the North and South Carolina Conference of the African Methodist Episcopal Church.

Reverend Nichols realized the importance of making his messages attractive and sought by every means at his command to do so. He was considered one of the most eloquent men at the conferences, and was in demand not only as a pastor but also at commencements and anniversary occasions.

Through the years he accumulated a good working library. Though the Bible was his favorite text, he enjoyed reading ancient history. Among the secret orders he identified with were the

Masons and the Odd Fellows. His main property interests were in Charleston. While his main residence was in Charleston, where he served as pastor of the Emanuel A.M.E. Church, one of the city's most important churches, Reverend Nichols and his family spent weekends and summers in Lincolnville.

Though family records indicate his ownership of three parcels of land in Lincolnville, only two lots have been accounted for. He may have donated one of them to Ebenezer A.M.E. Church, as his name is carved on one of the cornerstones of that church. The information on the cornerstone indicates that at the time of its dedication, 1903, he was the presiding elder of the district in which the church is located.

Reverend Nichols served as the first mayor (at that time the position was called intendant) of Lincolnville. In fact, the *Charleston News and Courier* identified him as mayor in the aftermath of the earthquake of 1886, three years before the town was incorporated. Records do not show how long he served.

Reverend Nichols died April 8, 1938, at his Charleston home, 70 Ashe Street. His wife predeceased him by a year. Their bodies are entombed at Emanuel A.M.E. Church in Charleston. Their last surviving child was the Right Rev. Decatur Ward Nichols, prelate of the African Methodist Episcopal church. He died in 2005 at the age of 105.

Reverend Nichols's surviving grandchildren are: Ruffin N. Noisette (North Carolina); Maude K. Reid (Florida); Lurline M. Noisette, Gloria Noisette Howard, Helen B. Noisette and Bettye Joe Noisette, all of Summerville; Wardean Nichols Henry (Huntington, New York), and Sioux Nichols Taylor (Mount Vernon, New York).

Intendant Jesse Smith

Jesse Smith, the second intendant of Lincolnville, owned land adjoining the property that was purchased for the first church, Ebenezer A.M.E. Church. Jesse Smith's land was on the southeast side of the church's property and was also bounded on the east by land owned by Richard Harvey Cain.

Intendant A. Tony Williams

A. Tony Williams, the third town intendant, bought a lot from Susan Owens and sold it to the town of Lincolnville. Williams Graded School was erected on this property. The cornerstone of the building indicates that it was constructed in 1899, the year the lot was purchased. Lincolnville was located in Berkeley County at this time. The school was named in honor of Intendant Williams. He allowed for "entertainments" to take place at the school, as long as the profits were used for renovating the school building, but after those expenses were covered he wanted to be sure than no such activities took place there. (See chapter on Lincolnville Elementary School.)

Records show that Williams was serving as intendant on April 31, 1899. E. K. Holman was clerk and treasurer. According to a town ordinance, two marshals served during the Williams administration.

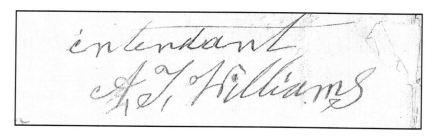

Signature of Intendant A.T. Williams

Intendant Williams died by 1902. His daughter, Emmaline A. Williams Mance, was an educator who taught at Alston Elementary School in Summerville for many years. His grandson, Clayton Mance, later became mayor of Lincolnville. His granddaughter is Mildred Mance Wigfall of Atlanta. His other grandsons were: P. J. Mance, who owned a successful business in Washington, D.C., for many years, and William Mance, an educator.

Intendant William Washington

According to town records, William Washington was the fourth intendant for the town of Lincolnville.

Intendant W. F. Hammond

W. F. Hammond was elected intendant in 1902, the fifth mayor of the town of Lincolnville.

Under the administration of Intendant Hammond, steps were taken to restrict activities considered detrimental to the quality of life in Lincolnville. He oversaw passage of the ordinance, requested by former Intendant Williams, limiting entertainments at the school. On April 15, 1904, he and the Town Council agreed that any person or persons known to be shooting within the corporate limits of the town or cursing or using abusive language on the public highway should be fined between $15.00 and $50.00, or that person could be sentenced to up to thirty days in the town

Signature of Intendant W.F. Hammond

jail. R. W. Nesbitt, town clerk and treasurer, witnessed the ordinance.

The following ordinance appears to have been presented in 1914, ratified in 1915, and received its third reading in 1916: "The ordinance states in part that any person or persons that is caught in the act of fast driving, fast riding or racing through the streets of the town, with a horse, mule or some other animal or with a machine of any kind, he, she, or they shall be arrested and brought before the proper tribunal for trial, and if found guilty of violating this ordinance, a fine of $5.00 to $10.00 shall be paid or be sent to the town lockup or county chain gang for 10 to 30 days." Intendant W. F. Hammond and J.W. Albright, clerk and treasurer, signed this ordinance.

In 1916 the town surrendered its town charter and became incorporated under the General Laws of the State of South Carolina. The resolution to accomplish this was introduced by R. Salters on May 3, 1916, and was adopted by the Town Council. Intendant W. F. Hammond and the town clerk C. E. Ladson signed the resolution.

Apparently for a time Intendant Hammond left his office and later returned to it, as he served both before and after Intendant William Seele, Sr.

Intendant William Seele, Sr.

The sixth intendant of Lincolnville was William Seele, Sr. The husband of Isabelle Seele, he was a member of Wesley Methodist Episcopal Church, a prominent church in the town, and superintendent of the church's Sunday School. He served as president of the Lincolnville Elementary School Parent Teacher Association. Records show that Mayor Seele served for a period of time in 1910.

Signature of Intendant William Seele, Sr.

Later, his brother, Charles Augustus Seele, and his son, William Seele, Jr., would also be elected to the position of intendant.

Following their administrations, William Seele, Sr., would be elected intendant two more times.

Intendant John Godfrey

John Godfrey, the seventh intendant for the town, lived on Pickens Street in Lincolnville. Not much is known about him, other than that he lived in a lovely cottage with many beautiful flowers and trees.

Intendant John Fennick

The eighth intendant was John Fennick. During his administration, the intendant and council passed ordinances dealing with keeping streets in the town clean, opposing shooting and cursing in the town, and raising the marshal's pay.

Intendant J.W. Albright

Not much is known about the ninth mayor, J.W. Albright. His previous service to Lincolnville included holding the position of clerk and treasurer in 1915 when W. F. Hammond was the intendant.

Intendant Pompey G. Lavally

Pompey G. Lavally, the tenth intendant of Lincolnville, was known as a gentle, kind-hearted person. His wife's name was Rosalee.

Many years after serving as intendant, he lived on Railroad Avenue in Lincolnville. When his wife died and he became ill, his neighbors Christopher and Anna Williams and their children cared for him. His granddaughter, Rosalee Prioleau, and a niece who lived in Georgetown came to visit him often. They finally took him to live in Georgetown after his prolonged illness.

Intendant Charles Augustus Seele

The eleventh intendant for the town was Charles Augustus Seele, brother of former intendant William Seele, Sr. He was married to Edna Seele, who lived to be 104. They had two children, Helene Seele Polk and Charles Seele, Jr.

Charles A. Seele was a member of Wesley Methodist Episcopal Church. He was a teacher of the Adult Sunday School class and secretary of the church. He was also a member of the Masonic lodge and an active civic worker.

Marshal Wilson served as the policeman during this administration. The wardens were W. F. Hammond, Hector Grant, Richard A. Ready, and Daniel Ben Barron.

Intendant Charles Augustus Seele

Intendant William Seele, Jr.

William Seele, Jr., the twelfth intendant for the town, was the son of William Seele, Sr., and Isabelle Seele. He and his family lived on Broad Street in Lincolnville.

Intendant William Seele, Sr.

The thirteenth intendant for the town was William Seele, Sr. This was his second tenure as intendant for the town. It is believed that two of the wardens at this time were Charles A. Seele and Mose Jerome Washington.

Intendant Mose Jerome Washington

Intendant Mose Jerome Washington

Mose Jerome Washington was the fourteenth intendant of Lincolnville. He was also a local preacher at Ebenezer A.M.E. Church in Lincolnville. He served on the Steward Board at Ebenezer, and was financial secretary of the Elk Lodge in Summerville. He was a painter with special and unusual skills, including rag painting and sponge painting on interior walls.

Mose Washington, along with William Seele, Sr., and Charles A. Seele, Sr., were known also for their Sunday evening Round Table Forums, or debates, as they were called. The young people of the town were eager to attend and listen as they discussed biblical, social, and political issues.

Intendant Washington was married to Gertrude Sabb Washington.

Intendant William Seele, Sr.

Following Intendant Washington's term, William Seele, Sr., was elected intendant for the third time. He was the last to carry the title intendant. The title was then changed to mayor.

During Intendant Seele's third administration, Lincolnville Road (now Lincoln Avenue) was paved from Owen's Drive, four blocks to Miller's Grocery Store.

Records show that citizens serving as wardens during this time were Edmund Edwards, Samuel Keller, Samuel Frasier, and Christopher E. Williams. Ruth M. Ross served as town clerk.

The Cosmopolitan Civic League of Lincolnville purchased playground equipment and had it installed on the grounds

Intendant William Seele, Sr. (seated) with Mrs. Ruth M. Ross, clerk. Standing left to right: Samuel Keller, Edmund Edwards, Christopher Elijah Williams.

of the old Town Hall (the former Williams Graded School) during this administration.

Marshals serving during Mayor Seele's administration were George Gardner, George White (1953), and Sam Bennett (1954-1967).

Mayor George Clayton Mance

The sixteenth mayor of Lincolnville was George Clayton Mance. He received his professional training at the Mortuary School of Embalming in Atlanta, Georgia. He worked at A. A. Aiken's Funeral Home in Summerville. Mayor Mance was the grandson of A. Tony Williams, the third mayor of Lincolnville. He had one daughter, Georgette Mance Stewart, and one son, Clayton Mance, Jr.

Mayor George Clayton Mance

Citizens serving along with Mayor Mance were wardens Clay Aiken, Curtis Glover, Samuel R. Cox, and Richard Drayton. Ruth M. Ross was the clerk, and Sam Bennett was the marshal. Curtis Glover served as chairman of the Finance Committee. Mayor Mance left office before the end of his term due to ill health.

Mayor Clay Aiken

Clay Aiken, the seventeenth mayor of Lincolnville, served for a short period of time, completing the term of Mayor Mance. He did not run for a second term. Some of the citizens who served as wardens during Mayor Aiken's administration were Curtis

Mayor Clay Aiken

Glover, Fred Noble, Sr., George Jacobs, and Richard Drayton.

Mayor Aiken was a very active member of Ebenezer A.M.E. Church. His professional trade was brick masonry. He was married to Bernice Aiken and they had five children.

Mayor Charles P. Ross

Charles P. Ross, our eighteenth mayor, was born on August 1, 1918, in Summerville. He was the son of Lillie Bell Ross Holman. His siblings are Mary Holman Tarver, Rev. Alonzo Holman, and Timothy Holman. He was married to the former Ida Brown.

Mayor Ross had strong work ethics and worked in a variety of jobs, including truck driver, taxi driver, lumber checker, longshoreman, and heavy equipment operator for the United States government.

Mayor Ross was a member of Ebenezer A.M.E. Church in Lincolnville, where he served as a member of the Trustee Board for many years. He had a long history of involvement in civic and political affairs.

Mayor Ross meets President Jimmy Carter

He was elected mayor for the first time in April 1967. Ross received the majority of votes, but his opponent Richard Drayton challenged the election, claiming that Ross had stood closer than 200 feet from the poll. The election was rescheduled. Guidelines were drawn up because there had been no rules in place to govern election proceedings for the town at that time. The next election was held in June 1967. Charles Ross won by a landslide along with four wardens: Herbert Cook, Willie Brown (who would die before his term ran out), George Jacobs, and Arnic J. Washington. Luella Doris Seele replaced Ruth Ross as clerk.

Sam Bennett, who had been the walking marshal during the administrations of Mayors Seele, Mance, and Aiken, continued to work until 1967. Charles Bell was hired as policeman for the town. The town's first police cruiser was purchased at this time, a 1965 Ford obtained from the South Carolina Highway Department. After two years of service, Herbert Cook resigned as warden, and F.A. Roberts was elected. Roberts was the first white man to hold this office in the town's history

It was during this time that Mayor Ross made his first of many mayoral contacts with U.S. Senator J. Strom Thurmond.

Mayor Ross believed that membership in the South Carolina Municipal Association was as beneficial to small towns as it was for large cities. Ross and two councilmen, F.A. Roberts and Arnic J. Washington, represented the town at the association's 29th annual meeting. The three officials met with Senator Thurmond and listened to an address by Vice President Spiro T. Agnew.

Politically, Mayor Ross claimed to be independent. He explained his position forcefully: "Lincolnville comes first in my book, Charleston County comes second, South Carolina third, and the United States fourth. The man who helps us progress in Lincolnville, I don't care if he's Independent, Republican, or Democrat – I'll support him."

After two years of service, F. A. Roberts completed his elected term as warden and decided to run for mayor. Ross defeated him. When Charles Ross was elected for a second term, the following citizens were elected to serve with him for four years: Samuel Cox, Harold Douglas, George Jacobs, and Arnic J. Washington.

After being elected for a second term, Mayor Ross continued his membership in political and civic associations and joined many others. Some of his political affiliations were with the Municipal Association of South Carolina, the National Conference of Black Mayors, and the South Carolina Conference of Black Mayors. He was also a member of the Charleston-Berkeley-Dorchester Council of Governments, the County Municipal Association, and several other civic and civil-rights organizations.

Mayor Charles P. Ross

Mayor Ross's tenure as Lincolnville mayor won wide acclaim. During his administration funds were secured to construct a recreation complex and the fire department was organized. The Lincolnville Elementary School property was bought and converted into a municipal building for the town. The Civic League installed street signs. The town had wrought iron railing designed by famed Charleston blacksmith Philip Simmons installed on the front porch of the municipal complex building. Almost 200 acres of land were annexed to the original town boundary, adding 125 citizens to the town's population.

Mayor Ross was respected on both the state and federal levels. He was invited to participate in White House conferences by Presidents Richard Nixon, Jimmy Carter, and Ronald Reagan.

In June 1970 Nathaniel P. Hardee was hired as policeman. Rosalee W. Washington served as acting clerk for two months, until Vermel B. Glover was hired as town clerk. When Glover resigned because of her relocation to another area, Washington again filled the role of acting clerk. In October 1971 Levi Duberry, Jr., was hired as town clerk.

Mayor Ross along with the councilmen decided to apply for a bloc grant to install a water system for the town. He approached two citizens, Rosalee Williams Washington and Christine Williams Hampton, to write a proposal for this project. The proposal was accepted and construction of a part of the water system was started.

Mayor Ross and the Town Council were also instrumental in bringing to Lincolnville the Jobman Caravan, a part of the Civil Service Interagency Council. This agency helped train students for government jobs. Mail service was switched from Lincolnville Circle to curbside service on each street. Election laws changed so that the mayor and Town Council candidates would be elected to four-year terms from a full slate. New town codes were put in place.

Mayor Ross requested $11,800 from Charleston County to help complete the fire station and to help provide police protection in the town. The request was denied because Charleston County Council could not determine whether this could be considered a loan or a gift, and the station wasn't completed until May 1979.

In 1974, thanks to a bill introduced in the General Assembly by Rep. Robert Woods, the town's governing body was changed from a mayor and four councilmen to a mayor and six councilmen.

Russ Cooper and Leroy Myers, Jr., were hired as police officers. Kay Tager served as chairperson of finance.

The next to challenge Mayor Ross was Betty Seabrook Hardee in 1971. Some of the citizens running on her slate were Leola P. Holmes, F. A. Roberts, and Josh Bell. Mayor Ross and his slate of candidates were elected. The election was challenged and a hearing was held in front of William Montgomery. Bernard Fielding, Esq., was town attorney, while the plaintiffs were represented by Attorney Thomas Broadwater. All charges brought

THE STATE OF SOUTH CAROLINA

BY THE SECRETARY OF STATE

WHEREAS, the municipality of _the Town of Lincolnville, S. C.,_ is incorporated under the laws of the State of South Carolina.

AND WHEREAS, a charter has been issued to the above municipality of the Town of Lincolnville, S. C. (Dec. 24, 1889).

AND WHEREAS, Section **47-26** of the 1962 Code of Laws, as amended, requires that all municipalities to adopt a specific form of government.

AND WHEREAS, an ordinance was filed with the Secretary of State on _August 23, 1976_, setting forth:

FIRST: The name of the municipality is _the Town of Lincolnville, S. C._

SECOND: The form of government adopted is _Mayor-Council_ form of government.

NOW THEREFORE, I, O. Frank Thornton, Secretary of State, by virtue of authority vested in me by section **47-28** of the 1962 Code, as amended, do hereby issue to the municipality of _the Town of Lincolnville, S. C.,_ this Certificate of Incorporation with the privileges, powers and immunities, and subject to the limitations prescribed in Act. No. 283 of 1975.

GIVEN under my Hand and Seal of the State, this the _23rd_ day of _August_ in the year of our Lord one thousand nine hundred and _76_, and in the two hundred and _1st_ year of the Independence of the United States of America.

Secretary of State

Form of Government
Mayor's Council
1976

by the plaintiffs were dismissed and Mayor Ross and the council were installed. Councilman George Jacobs was elected mayor pro-tem by the council.

Zelma Fielding was hired as clerk treasurer when Levi Duberry, Jr., resigned because of a job transfer. Councilmen at this time were Samuel Cox, Harold Douglas, George Jacobs, Kay Tager, Arnic J. Washington, and Joe Weaver.

In 1975 a room in the Town Hall was converted to a library. Civic League President Rosalee W. Washington requested that Town Council install shelves, so books would be accessible for children. Before renovation, the room, to the left of the entrance, had held first aid supplies. At the February 1976 meeting councilman Arnic J. Washington asked that an Election Commission be formed. It was agreed to form this committee with five members.

On March 3, 1976, the mayor and council discussed the form of government they would select. After much discussion, Rosalee W. Washington made a motion to retain the form of government presently in place. This motion was unanimously accepted. On April 7, 1976, Mayor Ross conducted the final reading on accepting the mayor-council form of government.

In 1977 Leo Pavlovich was hired as policeman and William Montgomery served as superintendent of streets. On April 4, 1978, Norman Craven was elected councilman to replace Kay Tager. In May 1978, Arnic J. Washington was elected mayor pro-tem.

Election laws were amended so that three councilmen would be elected every two years. This would insure that there would always be experienced people on council.

In 1978 the foundation for the fire station on Smith Street was readied, and the building was completed by the volunteer firemen in May 1979. It was made from the materials of an old building donated to the town by the General Electric Company of Ladson, South Carolina.

In 1979 the Civic League had the furnace in Town Hall repaired and the bathroom and kitchen were plumbed. On July

17, 1979, Lincolnville School property was deeded to the town for $1.00.

Councilmen at this time were George Jacobs, Samuel Cox, Joe Weaver, Norman Craven, Leroy Daniels, and Arnic J. Washington.

In 1980 Mayor Ross and Council discussed the feasibility of having a directional sign placed on Highway 78 for the town of Lincolnville. They also planned the swearing-in ceremony for council members Norman Craven, Leroy Daniels, Charles Duberry, Leland Shannon, Arnic J. Washington, and Joe Weaver.

Councilman Washington was again elected mayor pro-tem. Attorney Anthony O'Neil, Esq., served as town attorney, and Zelma Fielding was the town clerk.

In January 1982 Mayor Ross talked about resigning but later rescinded that decision. Though he had already served seventeen years, he was still thinking of other things he wanted to accomplish for the town. He especially wanted to raise $250,000 to complete the water system in all areas of the town. He also wanted to get a grant to upgrade the drainage system and put in a sewage system. Councilmen at the time were Tyrone Aiken, Charles Duberry, George Jacobs, Leland Shannon, Leroy Daniels, and Arnic J. Washington.

In 1984 the councilmen were Tyrone Aiken, Leroy Daniels, Alfred Baylock, Mary Williams, Annette Goodwin, and Charles Duberry. Due to the resignation of Leroy Daniels, a special election was held in August 1985, and James Hampton was elected to council.

In November 1984, Mayor Ross and fifteen other black mayors toured Hong Kong and the Republic of China representing the National Conference of Black Mayors and the United States Department of State.

Some other accomplishments during Mayor Ross's administration were: Installation of natural gas lines and cable TV, purchase of four fire trucks and three police cruisers, organization of a day care center, establishment of a municipal court, use of Charleston County dispatchers, remodeling of Town Hall with a

$250,000 grant, installation of fire hydrants, and construction of a lighted ball park

The final year of service for Mayor Ross was 1988. He always expressed the fact that he was working for "The Good of the Town." He also regularly credited his six-member council, the ladies of the Civic League, and others who worked to achieve whatever successes the town accomplished. He was known to say, "Without the help of council, I can do nothing. My hands are tied, I'm just their representative." Those councilmen during his last term were Tyrone Aiken, Charles Bell, Tommy Skinner, Charles Duberry, Alfred Baylock, and James Hampton. Hampton served as mayor pro-tem during Mayor Ross's last term.

Mayor Charles P. Ross died on July 20, 1989, at his home. He was eulogized on July 24 at his beloved Ebenezer A.M.E. Church in Lincolnville and buried at Brownville Cemetery in Summerville.

Mayor Ross served diligently as mayor of Lincolnville for twenty-one years.

Mayor Zelma R. Fielding

Zelma R. Fielding, the nineteenth mayor of Lincolnville, was elected in April 1988. She served one term. Previously, she held the position of town clerk during Mayor Charles Ross's administration. She was the first and only woman to serve as Lincolnville mayor.

Citizens serving on council with Mayor Fielding during her first two years in office were Tyrone Aiken, Charles Bell, Charles Duberry, Alfred Baylock, Tommy Skinner, and James C. Hampton. Sandra Lary was clerk and Officer Donnie White was policeman. Councilman Hampton resigned before the end of his term and Annette Douglas was elected to replace him.

In April 1989 David R. Hill presented a deed and title of the old cemetery (Bible Sojourn Society) to the town of Lincolnville. Records show that this cemetery dates back to July 31, 1889. It sits on 1.75 acres of land, which was originally part of the farm of Maria S. Eden. When the property was sold by Ms.

Mayor Zelma Fielding receiving a check for Hurricane Hugo damage.

Eden it was to be used as the Bible Sojourn Society Cemetery of Lincolnville. David R. Hill was a trustee. After the presentation of the deed and title to the town, Mayor Fielding stated that she hoped to develop the cemetery, but she was unable to accomplish this.

During Mayor Fielding's administration the town celebrated its 100th birthday on December 14, 1989. This centennial event brought about renewed pride and interest among citizens in the town.

Mayor Fielding was interested in continuing the work started by Mayor Charles Ross as well as taking on environmental issues. On December 1, 1989, the mayor sponsored an Arbor Day program in which she read a proclamation. Those assembled sang "Anthem for Arbor Day" (to the tune of "My Country 'Tis of Thee"), a tree was planted by William Montgomery, Jr., water commissioner, and Edward Simpson, Lincolnville fireman.

In December 1990 Councilwoman Annette Douglas resigned from the Town Council. Samuel Jacobs was elected to fill her spot. Councilman Duberry was elected mayor pro-tem and Enoch Dickerson was appointed to serve as municipal judge for the town.

In 1991 the Civic League sponsored the first Independence Day parade. This parade honored all active-duty Armed Forces personnel and those who had served previously in the military. Special tribute was given to servicemen returning from Operation Desert Storm.

Another event that was initiated by the Civic League during Mayor Fielding's term was the annual Christmas Tree Lighting Celebration. The tree was purchased and planted by the Civic League on the Town Hall grounds near the entrance of the building. The Civic League also started Pride Week, held in April each year, and selected the Yard of the Month. Mayor Fielding worked closely with the Civic League in these efforts.

Judge Enoch Dickerson put a Crime Watch organization into action. Hattie M. Salley, a citizen and member of the Crime Watch, was an outstanding worker in raising funds for this organization.

Mayor Fielding agreed to let the Civic League use the Town Hall's auditorium for the Summer Lunch program, which was restarted under the leadership of Rosalee W. Washington.

Councilmen serving during Mayor Zelma Fielding's final two years were Tyrone Aiken, Charles Duberry, Alfonzo Greene, Charles Buggs, Laverne Williams, and Leland Shannon. Alfonso Greene was elected mayor pro-tem.

Mayor Fielding was married to the late Timothy Fielding. They had one son, Mark Fielding.

Mayor Charles T. Buggs

Charles T. Buggs, twentieth mayor of Lincolnville, was born in Mississippi. He is the third of 14 children. He was educated in the public schools of Mississippi and Florida before serving in the military for 20 years. He retired from the United States Air Force in 1986 in Charleston, and decided to live in the area. A member of the Mount Moriah Baptist Church in North Charleston, he moved from Charleston to Lincolnville in 1983 and became active in the political affairs of the town. He was elected mayor in April 1992 as a write-in candidate.

The citizens serving on Town Council under Mayor Buggs during his two consecutive terms were Tyrone Aiken, Dorothy Bailey, Charles Bell, Andrew Carpenter, Charles Duberry, Alfonzo Greene, James C. Hampton, Ernest Jennings, Leland Shannon, Laverne Williams, and Sam Williams. Hampton and Greene served as mayors pro-tem at different times. Linda Grooms was clerk and Sonia Glover and Ernestine Devine served as billing clerk.

Mayor Charles T. Buggs

Mayor Charles Buggs's accomplishments during his tenure were projects that helped the town move forward. Some of these were: the extension of the natural gas line, improvement of the park and playground, upgrading of the financial status of the town to debt free, installation of additional street lights and a Lincolnville sign on Interstate 26, renovation of Town Hall, establishment of town-funded garbage pickup, establishment of a recycling center, and purchase of a fire truck and fire-fighting equipment, new computers, a copier, police radios, radars, police cars, and weapons. Streets were opened and paved. A big-screen television was purchased for the children to watch movies and educational programs at the Town Hall in the summer. A Senior Citizen Residential Complex was built. A Comprehensive Land Use Planning Committee was organized and work was started on the Zoning Compliance Committee. The grant to build the town's new Public Safety Building was obtained during Mayor Buggs's last administration.

In order to have more input from the citizens, Mayor Buggs also established a Mayor's Advisory Board. It was made up of Rosalee W. Washington, Mary Williams, J.B. Wagoner, Jean Weidman, and Mr. Phelps.

The following citizens worked for months on the Comprehensive Planning Committee: Christine W. Hampton, Rosalee W. Washington, Martina Jacobs, Roosevelt Brown, Barbara Dease, Jean Weidman, Dorothy Bailey, Laverne Williams, and Mary Howell. This committee worked under the guidance of several staff members from the Charleston County Office of Government.

Mayor Buggs worked with the Civic League as they continued to sponsor the Christmas Tree Lighting celebration. He assigned the planning of the Independence Day Parade to the Fire Department. During his last year in office the parade was canceled; though another celebration of the town's founders was expected to take place, this did not happen. In 1993 Mayor Buggs addressed many issues in his State of the Town Address. One very important issue was the sewer system, which had not been completed because the grant money was not enough to cover the entire town. However, town officials continued to seek additional funds until the job was completed.

The members of the Election Committee were John Connors, Jean Weidman, and Rosalee W. Washington.

On Sunday, December 12, 1993, a dedication service was held in memory of Mayor Charles P. Ross. The town's building and grounds were renamed The Charles Ross Complex. A sign honoring Mayor Ross was erected by the Crime Watch organization. The committee members for this ceremony were Tyrone Aiken, Charles Duberry, Judge Enoch Dickerson, Theodore Sellers, Zelma Fielding, Gladys Lincoln, Sonia Glover, and Chairperson Anna Williams Gleaton.

During the eight years that Mayor Charles T. Buggs served the town of Lincolnville, the town made great strides as he worked with citizens to continue the growth of the town.

Mayor Buggs was married to Victoria Buggs, and they had two children.

Mayor Tyrone E. Aiken

Tyrone E. Aiken, the twenty-first mayor of Lincolnville, was born in Summerville. He is the second of four children born to Edward and Stella Aiken. He was educated at Lincolnville Elementary School and R. B. Stall High School in North Charleston.

He served in the military for three years of active duty and eight years reserve duty. He is an active member of the historic Ebenezer African Methodist Episcopal Church in Lincolnville, where he serves on the Trustee Board and sings in the Senior Choir.

Mayor Tyrone E. Aiken

Mayor Aiken became interested in the civic and political affairs of the town at an early age. He served as a volunteer fireman, and worked with the youth of the community. Later he decided to enter the political arena and was successfully elected for several terms as councilman.

Councilman Aiken served as chairperson of the Recreation Department and also as chairperson of the Health Department. After serving as councilman for many years, Councilman Aiken decided to run for mayor and was elected in April 2000.

During his tenure as mayor, Mayor Aiken along with council remodeled the auditorium of the Charles Ross Complex, planted a replacement Christmas tree, installed additional lighting at the entrance to the Town Hall, revised the zoning ordinance,

Mayor Tyrone E. Aiken and City Council. Seated left to right: Council members Anna Ruth Williams Gleaton, Dorothy Bailey, and Barbara Dease. Standing left to right: James C. Hampton, Leland Shannon, Mayor Tyrone Aiken, and Charles Duberry.

reorganized the Zoning Committee and Zoning Board of Appeal, constructed the Public Safety Building, installed sidewalks and additional street lights, and organized the Heritage Festival. Citizens serving on the Zoning Committee in 2002 were Chairperson Marshall Kelly, Vice Chairperson Rosalee W. Washington, Leverne Locklear, Fred Noble, Sr., Ruth Roberts-Shepherd, Laverne Williams, and Donavan Jordan.

Citizens serving on the Zoning Board of Appeal were Robert Cheverie, Roosevelt Brown, Sarah Deweese, Larry Brown, and Mary White.

The citizens who served on council with Mayor Aiken were James Hampton, Charles Duberry, Leland Shannon, Ernest Jennings, Dorothy Bailey, Anna R. Williams-Gleaton, and Barbara Dease. Charles Duberry and James Hampton served as mayors pro-tem at different times during this period of time.

Mayor Aiken and his wife Deborah are the parents of four children.

The authors were able to compile the information in this chapter from several sources. Louis Ruffin Noisette, the grandson of the town's first mayor, was very helpful. The 1956 thesis "A Study of Lincolnville, S.C.: A Negro Community," by Luella Seele, who once taught at Lincolnville Elementary School, provided much information, as did records at the Lincolnville Town Hall and elsewhere. Unfortunately, many gaps remain. The authors encourage anyone who can provide additional information to contact them.

Lincolnville Mayors

Lewis Ruffin Nichols
Jesse Smith
A. Tony Williams
William Washington
W. F. Hammond
William Seele, Sr.
W. F. Hammond
John Godfrey
John Fennick
J.W. Albright
Pompey G. Lavally
Charles Augustus Seele
William Seele, Jr.
William Seele, Sr.
Mose Jerome Washington
William Seele, Sr.
George Clayton Mance
Clay Aiken
Charles P. Ross
Zelma Fielding
Charles T. Buggs
Tyrone E. Aiken

The Great Lincolnville Earthquake

Among the ordeals which the town of Lincolnville has faced is the most destructive earthquake to hit the east coast of the United States. Though the quake of August 31, 1886, is often called "The Great Charleston Earthquake," it was actually centered closer to Lincolnville than to any other community. Lincolnville included about 500 residents at the time.

The official report of the government, written by Capt. Clarence Edward Dutton of the U.S. Ordnance Corps, includes this description:

"Lincolnville is a small village, situated between two and three miles southeast of Summerville. It contains a few hundred inhabitants, nearly all of them negroes. It has several well-built wooden cottages, and a large number of cabins, the dwellings of the poorest class of blacks. The violence of the shocks here was apparently a little greater than at Summerville, though the difference is so small that its existence may seem doubtful. A larger proportion of the buildings were wrecked, and in some instances the destruction was more thorough. The damages were for the most part of similar nature to those in Summerville, and indicated vertical movements of great power. A number of buildings were moved to a considerable distance. One house which was wrecked was supported on wooden posts, some of which were broken off, others forced down laterally, while several retained their positions. The house moved ten feet south and three and a half feet east. The upper part of its chimney was little injured, but the lower part was crushed into a pile of ruins. Two or three hundred yards northeast of this house another cottage was thrown five feet south and three feet east. Its chimney was collapsed in the same manner as the first one. On the other hand, many cabins and some cottages escaped serious injury, but they all showed that they had been subjected to violent vertical movement and also to horizontal swaying. The piles on which they rested were hammered into the ground and the inclosing earth at their lower ends was molded so as to leave annular spaces around them.

"Summerville and Lincolnville are the only villages within the epicentral tract."

On September 6 a group of Summerville residents formed a relief committee that soon agreed to provide care for some of the communities near Summerville, including Lincolnville. Among the "Provisions and Medicines" that were distributed was $7.50 for "Nursing at Lincolnville."

Rev. Lewis Ruffin Nichols served as intendant (mayor) at the time, though the town was not yet incorporated. After the quake, a Charleston newspaper account explained that because the population of Lincolnville consisted "largely of widows and their children," a group from the town traveled to Summerville to seek assistance. On September 9 the Summerville relief committee provided five tents, received from the Charleston relief committee, to earthquake victims of Lincolnville. Eventually, 101 Lincolnville homes were repaired with the assistance of the Summerville Relief Committee. Apparently most of the damage was relatively minor, as the only residents who received relief payments of more than $50.00 were Maria Eden, $163.50, and R. Anderson, $60.00. In addition, 99 other Lincolnville homes were repaired with final costs totaling $1,707.60, or an average of less than $20.00 apiece.

Lincolnville Elementary School

The founders of the town of Lincolnville knew the importance of a good education, so as the town was just beginning to develop the leaders made plans for a school

In 1875 Richard Harvey Cain, a founder of Lincolnville, sold a lot on Pinckney Street to Susan Owens for $25.00. The year that the town of Lincolnville was incorporated by the South Carolina General Assembly, 1889, Susan Owens sold her lot to A. Tony Williams, later an intendant, or mayor, of Lincolnville. The cornerstone of the building that housed the Williams Graded School indicates that the school was constructed on this site in 1899.

Between 1899 and 1902, Williams agreed to sell the property to the town of Lincolnville. However, he had firm ideas about how the school was to be used. In 1902 an ordinance was passed in accordance with Mr. Williams's wishes. It stated that, "the schoolhouse could be used for entertainment and the proceeds from all entertainments would go towards putting the same in shape for school purposes and after the greater part of the work was done to make the school comfortable for the children, then all other entertainment would cease forever." The final payment was made and the title conveyed to the town in 1906.

Williams Graded School cornerstone

Tracking the deed for the property of the Williams Graded School reveals the following:

- Deed from Walter Steele to Richard Harvey Cain: November 6, 1868;
- Deed from Richard Harvey Cain to Susan Owens: October 25, 1875;
- Deed from Susan Owens to A. Tony Williams: December 22, 1899.

Careful reading of this last deed indicates that an old building was present on the site when Mr. Williams purchased it. It is also believed that this old building was used as the first school while Mr. Williams was building a new school.

Teacher Mattie Seabrook organized the new school, which was called the Williams Graded School. This school served the community until the area was incorporated into the Charleston County School System in 1923.

This one-story, high-gabled, rectangular, clapboard structure was used as the Town Hall after school hours. After a new school was built in 1924, the school built by Mr. Williams was used for many community activities, including serving as

The First Lincolnville School Building, believed to be the building on the lot purchased by A.T. Williams

Mattie Elizabeth Seabrook in 1899 (below left), pictured with Sadie Boags, the first teacher at Williams Graded School (right).

the Town Hall, until the fire station was built on Smith Street in 1979. Even then an office was set up in this building to conduct the business of the town. The former Williams Graded School was to be restored and used as a museum, and was even placed on the National Register of Historic Places in 1980. However, the building was destroyed by arson two years later.

Following the era of Mattie Seabrook (who later became Mattie Seabrook Hill), the following teachers served Lincolnville: David R. Hill (son of Mattie Seabrook Hill), Fanny Perry, G. Forrest, Ella Forrest, Gracie Ashe, Julia Mitchell, Emmaline A. Mance (daughter of A. Tony Williams), F. Patrick, and Grace Martin. These teachers received salaries of $20.00 a month.

When students finished the Williams Graded School, some of them commuted 25 miles by train daily to Charleston where they attended the Avery Institute on Bull Street. After graduating from Avery, many students attended either South Carolina State College in Orangeburg, Allen University in Columbia, or Claflin College in Orangeburg.

Lincolnville Elementary School

Lincolnville Elementary School, Circa 1945

Left to Right, 4th Row: Alonzo Holman, Jr, Clyde Hill, Roosevelt Williams, Thelma Keller, Rosalee Williams, Adonis Dezelle, Jr., Charles Deweese, Oliver Mack, Joseph Cuttino, Calvin Manley, Alice Williams, Mildred Daniels, Sarah Dezelle, unidentified, William Cuttino, Mary Mack, Mildred Muldrew, Freddie Hardee, Clarence Williams, Alonza Salley.

3rd Row: Mary Ellen Keller, Hazel Goode, Thelma Muldrew, Eunice Manley, Rosalee Salley, Edith Hill, Katrina Brown, Maria Goode, Lucille Rowe, Louise Keller, James Wilson, Richard Hardee, Leon Mack, Simon Admore, Gordon Hill, Leroy Daniels, Herbert Daniels, Lavonce Smith.

2nd Row: Leon Salley, Margaret Muldrew, Earl Doyle, Timothy Holman, Christine James, unidentifed, Essie Mae Williams, unidentifed Cuttino, Harold Goode, Earnestine Bennett, Bobby James, unidentified, Franklin Cuttino, Herbert Williams, John Douglas, Jr., Harold Douglas, Wilbur Harrison, Daisy Cuttino, Edward Daniels, Theodosia Bryant, unidentified, Willlie Williams, unidentified.

1st Row seated: Johnnie Gale, Mildred Carroll, Barbara Mance, Jean Daniels, William Mance, Jr., I.D. Carroll, Alvoronie Brown, Constance Goode, unidentified Gordon, William Muldrew, Sam Carroll, Jr.

Faculty: Mrs. Carrie Lou Aiken, Mr. E.P. Wooten (Principal), Mrs. W.A. Barron.

In 1924, a wooden structure was built on four acres of land on Broad Street. It consisted of four classrooms, an office, a kitchen, first aid room, and auditorium. It was built with funds provided by the Julius Rosenwald Fund, started by the founder of Sears, Roebuck, & Co., and so was called a Rosenwald School. The Rosenwald Fund built thousands of schools for black children throughout the South; the second largest number were located in South Carolina. The Rosenwald Fund spent almost $3 million building 500 schools for 74,000 black students in South Carolina between about 1917 and 1931. The teachers who taught in this wooden structure were: Blanche Gravely, Gladys Schutt, Mable Buddin, Naomi Grant, Rev. P. C. Henderson, Mattie Wilkins, F. C. Jackson, Annette Jackson, Etta Wilson, J. T. (John Thomas) Wilson (who later became principal of the Bonds-Wilson High School in Charleston), B. Frieson, C. I. Young, S. Wigfall, and E.P. Wooten.

The original Rosenwald School was completely remodeled with brick in 1953. It then consisted of four classrooms, a kitchen, office, large library, three restrooms, large auditorium, teacher's lounge, book room, and utility room. The school still was located on Broad Street in a pine grove and now had a lovely front flower garden. There were two drinking fountains in the building and

Original Lincolnville Elementary School built 1924

flood lights on each corner of the building. The classrooms were equipped with individual lockers, a reading corner, blackboards, maps, and globes. The building had a central heating system and running water. The total enrollment was 125 students. When the new school was occupied, Charleston County furnished the necessary supplies. The kitchen was equipped with a gas stove.

After completing elementary school, Negro students walked three miles to Summervilllle in Dorchester County to attend Alston High School. White students were transported by bus to North Charleston High School. Later in 1950, a private bus owned and driven by Esau Jenkins, a great civil-rights leader from Johns Island, was contracted to transport black students to Bonds-Wilson High School, in the Accabee section of Charleston.

Athletics were an important part of the educational programs at Lincolnville Elementary School. Intramural tournaments were held in basketball, baseball, and marbles. The Lincolnville teams were always immaculately dressed. Majorettes, dressed in blue and gold uniforms with hats and white boots, performed at halftime of basketball games. The Lincolnville teams won many medals and trophies, especially in basketball. Lincolnville Elemenary had the honor of producing some of the best marble shooters in the state of South Carolina.

The Parent-Teacher Association (PTA) sponsored many programs at the school. Each year the PTA put on a tea with a national theme and brought in a speaker to discuss various nationalities. Members held activities to raise funds for the school. They purchased uniforms for the basketball teams, books for the library, and plants and flowers for the campus.

Lincolnville Elementary majorette uniform

"Negroes On Parade" program cover

Meetings were held monthly and were very well attended. Programs were carefully planned for PTA meetings and refreshments were served after each meeting.

Some of the faculty members who taught in the new brick school were: Carrie Lou Aiken, Louella Seele, Geraldine Fields, Paul Abraham, and Doris Watson. Wilhemenia Barron was the principal and also taught seventh grade. After the death of Mrs. Barron, Eugene Willis became principal. Other teachers were: Margaret Boone, Nellie Mayes, Leila Britton, Rosalee W. Washington, Lucille Noble, and Grace Hunt.

Many wonderful activities and events took place in the brick school. A weekly assembly program was held every Friday morning in the auditorium. The first grade teacher, Carrie Lou Aiken, played music on the piano as the classes marched in and out of the auditorium in an orderly manner.

The annual Black History Program was a very special event. Students portrayed famous black people, dressing as that person and reciting a speech by his or her character or telling the story of that person's life.

Another annual school event was the speaking contest. The winners participated in the Charleston County District Level Contest.

The annual Halloween party was always a fun time for children and parents. The entire family took part. Some of the games were bobbing for apples, pin the tail on the donkey, and darts. The students and teachers dressed in costumes. Each year there was a Thanksgiving celebration. The students brought canned goods to put in baskets for those in need. The choir sang beautifully. The students always looked forward to Christmas at

Lincolnville Elementary School. There was a beautiful tree in the auditorium, and a present for each child under the tree. The children also received bags of fruit.

Being in the school's choir was an honor for the students. Teacher Carrie Lou Aiken, an excellent musician, directed the choir. The girls wore black dresses with large white collars. The boys wore black pants, white shirts, and black bow ties. The voices blended together beautifully and the students looked wonderful.

At the end of the school year, three important events were held at Lincolnville Elementary School. The first was May Day.

James Allen Williams, Speaking Contest 2nd place winner, 1962

The teachers and students practiced for weeks and decorated the building and playground. Everyone especially looked forward to the wrapping of the Maypole with streamers. The girls wore beautiful dresses and the boys were handsomely dressed. It was a joyful day.

The second big event for the end of the year was the school-closing play, sometimes referred to as the "Operetta." Every grade took part in this full production with costumes and scenery. The students and teachers practiced for weeks before the grand production. The students always performed well and the auditorium was filled to capacity with parents, faculty, students, and visitors.

The last event for the school year was the seventh-grade graduation ceremonies. Everyone in the community came to witness these important activities. The Commencement exercise was held on a Friday in the auditorium with the entire student body, parents, and friends present. The honored students who had

Graduation day 1960. Anna Ruth Williams dressed for the ceremony with her father's car in the background.

earned the positions of valedictorian and salutatorian delivered addresses. This was followed by the more formal Baccalaureate Ceremony held on Sunday. Graduates were proud as they reached this first milestone in their educational journey. As Carrie Lou Aiken played the beginning chords for "Pomp and Circumstance," the students stood at attention. A speaker delivered words of encouragement. The girls dressed in beautiful white dresses with pastel-colored cummerbunds and a corsage. The boys dressed in white pants, navy blue or black jackets, ties, white shirts, and dark shoes. It was an exciting day for students and parents alike.

The Lincolnville Elementary School was a very important part of the community. It closed as a school in 1969 due to the integration of the Charleston County School System.

Graduation Day 1949
back: Freddie Hardee, Charles Deweese,
front: Mildred Muldrew, Rosalee Williams.

Lincolnville Elementary graduating class of 1950. Standing (l to r): Herbert Williams, Harold Goode, Calvin Manley, Earl Doyle, Clarence Williams, and John Squire. Seated (l to r): Thelma Keller, Sarah Dezelle, and Alice Williams.

From that time, the students from Lincolnville were sent to Ladson Elementary School.

The Lincolnville Elementary School was deeded to the town on July 17, 1979. It was converted into the Town Hall under the leadership of Mayor Charles Ross. The old, wooden Lincolnville Elementary School is now known as the Charles Ross Municipal Complex, still serving the community as it has for many decades.

Lincolnville Elementary School today

The Annual Educational Sermon

Lincolnville Elementary School
Lincolnville, South Carolina

Sunday May 18th, 1958
At Four-thirty O'Clock in the Afternoon

PROGRAMME

PROCESSIONAL .... "God of Our Fathers"
Hymn ...... "Lead On, O King, Eternal" .... Glee Club
Invocation .. Rev. M. S. Freeman, Pastor, Bethel A.M.E. Church, Summerville
Anthem .... "Praise Ye The Father!" .... Glee Club
Presentation of Speaker ... Rev. Wm. Seale, President, Lincolnville P.T.A.
SERMON .... REV. JAMES E. COOK
Pastor, Baum Temple A. M. E. Zion Church, Summerville
Duet ..... "Whispering Hope" .. Ramonia Pinckney & Victoria Douglas
ANNOUNCEMENTS
Benediction ... Rev. Josh Gadsden, Pastor, Ebenezer A.M.E. Church
RECESSIONAL ....

CLASS ROLL:

BARNES, Martha Nancy;   CAMPBELL, Wilhelmenu;   DOUGLAS, Victoria
    PINCKNEY, Ramonia;   SHANNON, Marion;   WILLIAMS, Christine.
BAMBERG, Curtis;   DEZELLE, Solomon;   DOUGLAS, Aaron;   FIELDS, Joseph Nathan
    GORDON, Alfred Leroy;   GRANT, Edmond
HOLMES, Volney;   STEPHENS, Joseph;   WATSON, Henry.

Class Motto: "Forward Ever, Backward Never!"
Colors: Pink and Green.   Flower: Glomelia

FACULTY:
Mrs. C. L. Aiken,   Mrs. G. R. Fields   Mrs. M S. Boone
Mrs. L D. Seele.   MRS. W. A. BARRON, PRINCIPAL

Lincolnville Elementary School Song

Dear Lincolnville we love you so
A tribute song we raise, we'll work
For you till victory's won
And give you lots of praise.

Hurrah for dear old Lincolnville
Hurrah for school days here
Hurrah for alma mater still
And thoughts of you so dear.

Dear Lincolnville we are loyal
Sons and ever shall remain. We'll
Work for you till victory's won
And friends for you we'll gain.

Hurrah for dear old Lincolnville
Hurrah for school days here
Hurrah for alma mater still
And thoughts of you so dear.

Lincolnville Churches

Ebenezer African Methodist Episcopal Church

The history of Ebenezer A.M.E. Sunday School and church dates back to the beginning of the town of Lincolnville. On November 6, 1869, A.M.E. minister Richard Harvey Cain, William Eden, and Marc Buffett signed the deed for the purchase of land for the first church in the village. According to the deed of conveyance, the land was purchased from Walter Steele of Charleston, and included 45 feet of frontage on Pinckney Street, running back about 100 feet to a lot owned by Jesse Smith on the southeast side. The church land was also bounded on the east by Reverend Cain's property.

Ebenezer A.M.E. Church (1878-1960)

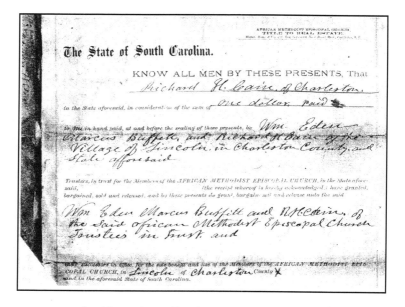

Deed for purchase of land for Ebenezer A.M.E. Church

The church that would become known as Ebenezer African Methodist Episcopal Church was built on this land in 1878, under the leadership of Reverend Cain, who at that time lived in Charleston. Originally a meeting house for prayer and class meetings, the church was founded and to a great extent built by many of the same men who founded Lincolnville itself. Its history and that of the town, especially in their early years, are closely entwined. The original sills for the building were hewed by Marc Buffett, George Duffy, and David Hines, Sr.

Among the early presiding elders were Lewis Ruffin Nichols, P. J. Chavis, and E. H. Colt. Each of these men played a part in carving the history of the church.

In 1880 Reverend Cain joined the church to the African Methodist Episcopal denomination. In 1886 the first pastor, Rev. Elias J. Gregg, was assigned to lead the church.

Following Reverend Gregg was Reverend Ransom. During his administration a porch was added to the church. Bethel A.M.E. Church in Summerville was joined to Ebenezer to form a circuit. After Reverend Ransom, the following pastors served

Ebenezer A.M.E. Senior Choir (l to r): Daniel Ben Barron, Ida Ross, unidentified, Mary Kitt, Emmaline Mance, Wilhemenia A. Barron, Rev. Roosevelt Brown.

the circuit: Rev. C. W. Mance, Reverend Lucas, who died soon after receiving his calling, and Reverend Ladson.

Joseph Grant was the first organist of Ebenezer A.M.E. Church. At the time he served, Mrs. Lenear, M. S. Sparks, Christine Brown, and Susan Hammond were members of the choir.

Ebenezer's first remodeling was accomplished under the pastorate of the late C. W. McQueen in 1903. The cornerstone was laid at that time. As time went on, the old patriarchs recognized the need to improve the organization of the church. They drew up rules and regulations for the governing body of the church. Then came the Rev. B. A. Bianchi and Rev. C. W. Mance for the second time. Some of the pastors who followed Reverend Mance in 1917 were: Rev. P. C. Lee, Rev. S. Ball, Reverend Rhames, and Reverend Enoch. During Reverend Ball's tenure, the floor was carpeted for the first time.

In 1928 Rev. W. K. Wilson served as pastor. He began raising funds to move the choir from the front entrance area to the space behind the pulpit. The church was then joined to the Goose Creek Parish. Rev. L. L. Farmer led the membership in making repairs to the roof. The church was joined to the Saint

Luke A.M.E. Church in the Bacon Bridge area of Summerville in 1930 during Reverend Farmer's pastorate.

Following Reverend Farmer came Rev. S. D. Brown, Rev. E. W. Graham, Reverend Nero, and Rev. Jessie Middleton. Reverend Middleton had a beautiful voice and loved to sing the song "Wonderful Words of Life." In 1944 he worked faithfully to lead the congregation in placing the choir in its present position behind the pulpit and he carpeted the pulpit area. He was moved to another assignment before the choir loft could be dedicated, so in 1945 the dedication was performed by Rev. Roosevelt Brown. The completion of the work started by Reverend Middleton constituted the second remodeling of Ebenezer A.M.E. Church.

During Reverend Brown's assignment at Ebenezer many auxiliaries were started to encourage the children not only to work in Sunday School, but also to participate in the work of the church. One example of the groups started was the Red Club chaired by Mary Gardner. She organized a group of young people

Ebenezer A.M.E. Church Red Club circa 1949.
Top Row left to right: Rev. Roosevelt Brown, Alonzo Holman, Earl Brown, Clyde Hill; 2nd row: Mildred Carrol, Barbara Brown, Rosalee Williams, Mary Holman; Front row: Mary Gardner (President), Catherine (Kate) Edwards, Earl Doyle, Herbert Williams, Leroy Brown.

Standing front with sign:
Sylvia Greer; Seated: Mary H. Goldman, Rev. I.W. Bennett,
Rosalee Williams; 1st row standing: Daniel B. Barron, Rachel McCray, Alice Williams,
Naomi Squire, Christopher Williams; last row standing: Ruth Ross, Wilhemina A. Barron.

to work with her on programs to help the church's finances. During Reverend Brown's term at Ebenezer, Daniel Ben Barron became organist and choir director. He held these positions until his death. Dr. J. E. Beard was the speaker for the choir dedication service. His topic was "The People Had a Mind To Work"; all who heard it remembered this theme. The subject became a motto representing the spirit of the ministries as well as the congregation of Ebenezer A.M.E. Church from that time to the present.

Rev. Dan Curry was named the church's next pastor, followed in 1951 by Rev. I. W. Bennett. He too had a spirit for working and made many improvements. During his pastorate an electric organ was installed, which added greatly to the spirit of the worship services. Reverend Sweet was the next pastor to serve Ebenezer.

The spirit of work and cooperation among the members of the congregation continued when Rev. Josh William Gadsden came to serve, along with presiding elder B. H. Gray. Reverend Gadsden displayed his spirit of work through tireless efforts and great fortitude that was evident in bringing improvements and advancements at the church. In 1959, Reverend Gadsden held a meeting with the officers of the church. It was at this meeting that the suggestion of brick veneering the church was made and heartily approved. This set in motion another project for the improvement of the church. Through the efforts of the Pulpit Aid Board, Ida Brown Ross, president of the board, presented a lovely set of furniture to be placed in the pulpit area of the church.

Reverend Josh Gadsden

On October 30, 1960, all eyes were centered on the completion and laying of the cornerstone. During Reverend Gadsden's administration the church was brick veneered, the pews and pulpit set were purchased, the cornerstone laid, and a christening fountain in memory of W. A. Barron was dedicated. This was the third major improvement to Ebenezer.

After Reverend Gadsden came Rev. Rufus Cochran, followed by Rev. Ned I. Edwards, who worked faithfully to build a parsonage. During Reverend Edwards's administration a water fountain was purchased in memory of Miller and Ruth Ross, new collection tables were purchased in memory of Samuel Aiken and Samuel Frazier. Anna R. Williams, president of the Trustee Auxiliary Board, accepted the responsibility of raising funds for the church's insurance.

In 1975 Reverend George Corbin came to pastor Ebenezer Church. With his guidance and direction a new piano was purchased, central heating and air conditioning was installed, the pastor's study and choir room were carpeted, a new roof was added, and the ceiling repaired. New light fixtures were installed and the Usher Board, under the leadership of president Kate Edwards, contracted to have a mural painted on the wall behind the choir. Dorothy Glover presented the church with silver collection plates

Reverend George Corbin and the Ebenezer A.M.E. Church Senior Choir. Front Row (l to r): Anna Ruth Williams Gleaton, Bessie Linen, Alice R.W. Smith, Lottie Singleton, Stella Aiken. Back Row (l to r): Rev. George Corbin, Ida B. Ross, Edward Aiken, Ethel Cobin, Margaret Loggan, Lucille Noble.

and vases in memory of her husband, Curtis Glover. The Red Club, under the leadership of president Alice Williams Smith, donated new back doors. The Junior Choir, led by Stella Aiken, purchased new front doors. The parking lot of the church was also enlarged.

In 1986 Rev. Charles H. Brown was assigned to the pastorate of Ebenezer. Under his leadership, the church parsonage was completed and dedicated. The Bible Study sessions grew as Reverend Brown brought the Bible to life through his lively and inspirational teachings.

In 1988 Rev. Calvin Morris was assigned pastor of Ebenezer. During his tenure the framework for the educational facility was erected.

In 1990 Rev. Jeremiah McKinley became pastor. During

Reverend Jeremiah McKinley

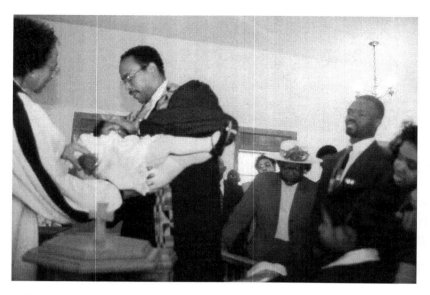
Rev. Isaac Johnson and Rev. Mildred Cox performing the christening of Morgan Jones.

his term the major portion of the interior of the educational wing of the church was completed.

In 1994 Rev. Isaac Johnson was assigned to serve at Ebenezer. During his stay the educational wing of the church was brick veneered. A new cornerstone was laid and the building was dedicated. A mortgage was acquired to pay for the work. Rev. Anna Williams, a local minister of the church, donated silver bread plates for communion in memory of her husband, Christopher Williams; Alethia Brown donated ten tables in memory of her husband, Charles F. Brown, Sr.; and Elizabeth Hill donated the carpet in memory of her husband, Gordon Hill, Sr. Bessie Linen donated the refrigerator in the kitchen of the educational building in memory of her mother Lottie Singleton and her husband Ralph Linen.

The Williams children—Rosalee, Alice, Clayton, Edmond, Christine, Anna Ruth, Sandy, and James—refurbished the library furniture in memory of their father, Christopher Williams, and in honor of their mother, Rev. Anna Williams. Christopher Williams was the leader of Class 9 for forty-two years; Rev. Anna Williams was recognized for her 30 years of ministerial work.

In 1997 the railings along the stairway of the educational building were installed in honor of Edward Aiken, donated by Tyrone Aiken and his family.

In 1988 the railing for the disabled was installed and dedicated. Bibles were given in memory of Maxine Stevenson, Christopher Williams, and Charles F. Brown, Sr. The Bibles were given by Rev. Levern Stevenson, Rev. Anna Ruth Williams Gleaton, and Alethia N. Brown.

Under the leadership of Rev. J. P. Cummings, Jr., members of the congregation paid off the mortgage in June 2001.

In 2001 the congregation was blessed to have Rev. Anna Ruth Williams Gleaton assist Reverend Cummings at Ebenezer during his extended period of illness. During the time Reverend Williams Gleaton assisted Reverend Cummings, the Bible study class grew in attendance.

The year 2002 brought a new pastor, Rev. E. T. Jones. During his stay at Ebenezer the church members celebrated 124 years in Christian service. There were also many other accomplishments for the church. Rev. Dr. Alonzo W. Holman, who grew up in Lincolnville, and his wife Gerald gave the padding around the altar. Reverend Holman served many years in the A.M.E. church, but never forgot his home church. Jackie Singleton presented

Ebenezer A.M.E. Church (1988 to Present)

the church with two microphones and an amplifier in memory of her husband, Ivory. Through the efforts of the Trustee Board and various members of the congregation, the altar, choir, and pulpit areas received a "makeover" to beautify the appearance of the sanctuary. The newly formed Daughters of Sarah, under the direction of Alice Williams Smith, purchased the pew ropes, pulpit candles and cross set, and coverings for the communion tables, and they cushioned the church pews. Bibles were donated to Ebenezer A.M.E. Church by Rosalee W. Washington, a member of the Home Church Class. James and Christine W. Hampton donated a picture of the Last Supper. The Missionary Board also donated a picture for the educational building.

Under the leadership of Christine W. Hampton, a member of the Trustee Board, a major restoration of the church took place. The 126-year-old knotty pine floor was refinished and the foundation stabilized, the electrical system and plumbing were upgraded, bathroom facilities were completely stripped and replaced, while new floors, cabinets, fixtures, and toilet units were installed. The heating and air conditioning were extended to the classrooms and to the kitchen area of the educational building. Fifty padded chairs were purchased for the dining area. The inside of the church and the outside trim were painted.

In February 2004 the educational building was renamed for Dr. Alonzo W. Holman, "Our Favorite Son."

The Ebenezer African Methodist Episcopal Church family continues to grow in the spiritual body of Christ. Their Motto is, "The People Had A Mind To Work."

Ebenezer A.M.E. Sunday School

In 1876, seven years after the land for Ebenezer African Methodist Episcopal Church was purchased, and two years before the church would be built, William Eden started a Sunday School in his home on the west side of the railroad station. Hector Grant served as his associate. Together they started the Ebenezer African Methodist Episcopal Church Sunday School, a vibrant program which continues to this day.

This little group made great progress with the children and soon others joined them. When Eden passed away, Grant became superintendent of the Sunday School. Hector Grant was a very energetic and farsighted superintendent.

Joseph Grant, son of Hector Grant, became the next superintendent. Serving along with him were many enthusiastic ladies and gentlemen. Some of the workers were: M.S. Sparks, Adrama Grant (sister of the superintendent), Katie Green, Professor David R. Hill (secretary), and Mattie Seabrook (treasurer), who later married Professor Hill. Joseph Grant made elaborate preparations for anniversaries and special days. He was a lover of music and his delight was to hear children sing. His assistant in music was Mary Miles Tobin, who also loved music. She demonstrated this by teaching new songs to the children for all occasions. Some of her favorite songs were "Sitting By the Gateway," "Oh Child of God Wait Patiently," "Why Not Now," and others.

The next superintendent was Professor David R. Hill. Professor Hill was a born teacher and leader. During his term the first banners were displayed and the library was started.

After Professor Hill's tenure, Joseph Grant became superintendent for a second time. He was still active, musical, and energetic. He was fortunate to have a cooperative group of workers who kept the Sunday School functioning during the winter quarters. Next in order came Elijah Bellamy, who was assisted by Miss Lucretia Brown.

The next superintendent was William Washington, who served under Rev. C.W. McQueen. He always had the pleasure of the children at heart as well as their religious training. The first piano was purchased during Brother Washington's administration. Professor Richard A. Ready was the first pianist, as well as assistant superintendent and musical director. "Good things do not last long," says the old adage, and Brother Washington's health failed. Because of this, T.A. Albright was chosen as the next superintendent. This lady was always business-like and alert. The children were ready at all times to be presented on any occasion. She was outstanding for programs and parties on short notices. She paid off the last installment on the piano. She attended many cultural affairs such as a concert at the Opera House in Summerville to

The Ebenezer A.M.E. Sunday School circa 1950. Seated (l to r): Christine Williams, Clayton Williams, Edmond Grant, I.D. Carroll, unidentified, Alvoronie Brown, Sam Carroll, Jr.; 1st row standing: Daniel B. Barron, supt, Mildred Carroll, Timothy Holman, Herbert Williams, Earl Doyle, unidentified, Rev. Roosevelt Brown; 2nd row standing: Rachel McCray, Barbara Brown, Catherine Edwards, Mary Holman, Rosalee Williams, Leroy Brown, Mary Kitt; 3rd row standing: Emmaline Mance, Charles H. Brown, Earl Brown, Clyde Hill, Ida Ross, Alonzo Holman, Wilhemenia Barron.

hear noted singer Sidney Woodward, at which she was one of the noted guests.

The Biblical admonition "Train up a child in the way he should go, and when he is old he will not depart" is true in the training of Daniel Ben Barron, who was the next superintendent. He was interested, energetic, and untiring in his work for the Sunday School. He was the first superintendent to accumulate a bank account for the Sunday School program. The second piano was purchased during his tenure. One special and modern piece of his work was the Sunday School grading system. Barron had very creative ideas for the Sunday School, including the use of a portable board where he made abstract drawings to coincide with the theme of the Sunday school lesson. The lesson was discussed and the children were given a chance to determine what the drawing represented.

Music was always an integral part of the Sunday School experience. It was even more pronounced under Daniel Barron's administration. He played the piano with such joy and enthusiasm that the children were drawn to Sunday School to listen, learn, and sing the songs he taught. Special days were particularly enjoyable for the children. Daniel Barron along with the teachers prepared programs such as plays, recitations, dialogues, and songs that complemented the theme of the programs. It was a joy for the children to memorize the speeches and songs.

During his administration many exciting and educational activities took place. Adults from Ebenezer A.M.E. Church and Wesley Methodist Episcopal Church in Lincolnville joined together on one Sunday evening of the month and conducted what was called a "Round Table Discussion" on a biblical theme. These discussions were very lively, informative, and entertaining. Members from both churches and the community attended these discussions. The young people of Ebenezer A.M.E. Church also had their own afternoon program, which was called The Allen Christian Endeavor League. This activity was well attended. The young people were taught the history of the church, spirit songs, and Bible lessons to go along with everyday living. It also provided time for the young people to socialize at the end of the spirit song and the "league clap."

One of the songs the young people loved was "A Song I'll Sing to You" or "The Church is Moving On," words by L. H. Coppin, and the tune by Robert Lowry. The lyrics provide a brief history of the A.M.E. Church, and the fifth verse specifically names Lincolnville founder Bishop Richard Harvey Cain:

> Of Turner next we sing,
> A mighty host did bring
> Of loyal men and women too,
> And Dickerson and Cain,
> Who did not long remain,
> Are resting with the tried and true.

Daniel Ben Barron worked for the Lord in the Sunday School and the church, and encouraged others to do so, too. His work portrayed his life and character. He was a Christian leader and a gentleman.

In 1936 members of the Sunday School staff were: Mary M. Kitt, Beginners; Emmaline Mance, Primary; Rachel McCray, Junior Boys; Hattie Frazier, Junior Girls; Mose Jerome Washington, Intermediates; Wilhemenia Barron, Senior Class; Professor David R. Hill, Adult; Hattie Frazier, treasurer; M. J. Washington, secretary; and Daniel Ben Barron, superintendent Rev. E.W. Graham served as pastor.

After the death of Daniel Ben Barron, his wife Wilhemenia became Sunday School superintendent. She picked up the torch passed on by her husband and continued the programs. She also started some new programs of her own. She was a born lover of children, and she worked diligently to improve the plans initiated by her husband.

During Wilhemenia A. Barron's time as superintendent she organized a group of substitute Sunday School teachers to work along with the regular teachers. In this way the young people were inspired to spend more time preparing their lessons for the class. Wilhemenia A. Barron also worked hard to increase the enrollment for the Sunday School. After five years of untiring service she was called from her labors to her reward. Some of the members of the Sunday School staff at this time were: Wilhemenia A. Barron, Emmaline Mance, Hattie Frazier, Rachel McCray, Ida Ross, Rosalee W. Washington, Alice Williams, and Edna Elaine Glover (substitute). Musicians were Alice Williams and Mildred Carroll.

Our next superintendent was Rosalee W. Washington. She received her training under the leadership of the superintendents Daniel Ben and Wilhemenia Barron and was well prepared when she was elected to serve as superintendent. She was a Christian worker, a public school teacher, and a patient and understanding person who knew how to plan, produce, and get the job done. One of her major accomplishments was to set aside Children's Day each year as promotion day in Sunday School. Rosalee W. Washington was also a lover of music and carried on the production of programs that incorporated many songs. The children were still required to memorize the words to songs and recitations, dialogues, and plays, as they prepared for special programs. Under her leadership, attendance grew. The interest and support of parents aided in the continued development of the Sunday School. Those who worked with her were: Edna Elaine Glover,

Sunday School group during the tenure of Rev. J.P. Cummings.

Beginners Class; Emmaline Mance, Primary Class; Rachel McCray, Junior Class; Ida Brown Ross, Intermediate Class; Rosalee W. Washington, Senior Class; Rev. Mose J. Washington, Adult Class; Lucille Noble, cradle roll; Gail Glover, secretary; Alice W. Smith and Lucille Noble, musicians; Ruth Ross, treasurer; and Shirley Skinner and Anna Ruth Williams, substitute teachers. Rev. Josh Gadsden was pastor of the church.

The next superintendent was Fred Noble, Sr., who still serves in this position. Fred Noble is a faithful worker who believes in promptness. His years as superintendent probably exceed all other superintendents of Ebenezer's Sunday school.

His workers at the beginning of his administration were Christine W. Hampton, assistant superintendent; Fred Noble, Senior Class; Ida Brown Ross, Intermediate Class; Elaine Glover, Junior Class; Lee Esther Aiken, Primary Class; Gail Glover and Rochelle Aiken, Beginners Class. Rev. Ned I. Edwards served as pastor.

Other workers during his long tenure were: Georgia Kelly, Elizabeth Hill, Lucille Noble, James Hampton, and Juanita Noble. Musicians were Lucille Noble, Alice Smith, Fred Noble, Jr., and Fred Noble III.

At left (l to r): Nicole Simmons, Jade Hampton and Katura Simmons. Below: Ryan Carpenter and Jade Hampton.

The following pastors served during this time: Rev. Rufus Cochran, Rev. Ned I. Edwards, Rev. George Corbin, Rev. Charles Brown, Rev. Calvin Morris, Rev. Jeremiah McKinley, Rev. Isaac Johnson, Rev. J.P. Cummings, and Rev. E.T. Jones.

The Sunday School remains an integral part of the spiritual life of the church. It is the foundation on which the church is based.

Members wearing "Team Shirts" on Unity Day

Sunday School members, 2000

Wesley Methodist Episcopal Church

During the early settlement of Lincolnville, a group of men and women from Centenary Methodist Episcopal Church in Charleston had a vision to organize a Methodist church in Lincolnville. They encouraged some of the settlers to start a Sunday School in the home of John Gibbs, a local preacher. S. J. Smalls was elected superintendent. Some of the other founders of the Sunday School were Peter Miller, another local preacher, and William Frasier.

The attendance at the Sunday School grew so large that more space was needed. A wooden building was erected and the Wesley Methodist Episcopal Church was started on Front Street. The pastor was Rev. C. F. Jacobs. The earliest records of this church date back to 1887, according to the date inscribed on the oldest cornerstone of this building. Unfortunately, much of the history of this church has been lost, especially by a house fire.

The Wesley Methodist Episcopal Church

The wooden structure was built to accommodate a small membership. The choir loft was located behind the pulpit. In later years a beautiful pipe organ was placed in the front right corner of the church. A potbelly heater was placed midway in the church on the left side. This heater was later replaced by a gas heating system.

Members of the Wesley congregation worked closely as a church family. One project which they labored to complete was the purchase of a large crystal chandelier. Records show that the lamp originally was illuminated by kerosene. Later, the members converted it to electricity. This chandelier still hangs in the church.

The Wesley Methodist Episcopal chandilier (left) and the church organ (below).

Some of the dedicated members in the life of the church during the years 1940-1967 were: William and Isabelle Seele, Sr. and family, Charles A. and Edna Seele, Sr., Helene Seele, Charles A. Seele, Jr., Luella D. Seele, Pernessa Seele, Janie Rowe, Mary Bowman, Samuel and Mammie Keller and family, Emily Goode and family, Sam Bennett and family, Mary Mack and grandchildren, Nathan and Elouise Daniels and family, Gertrude Washington, William and Anna Muldrew and family, Susie Brown and family, Edmund and Anna Edwards, Edna Edwards, and Ruth Keller.

Records show that the following ministers served at Wesley Methodist Episcopal Church: Rev. W. R. Jervay, Reverend Mingo, Rev. M. P. Pyatt, Rev. William C. Strother (1940), Rev. B. C. M. Wilson, Reverend Bowens, Rev. Ernest Newman, Reverend Spears, Rev. James S. Gadsden, Rev. L. T. Jackson, Rev. J. V. Livingston (1963), Reverend Generette, and Rev. J. V. Livingston (1967).

In 1967 Wesley United Methodist (formerly Wesley Methodist Episcopal) Church was closed due to the decline in membership. The remaining members then joined in membership at Wesley United Methodist Church in Summerville.

Several years later the scouts from the movie *Queen* came to Lincolnville to consider this church as a site for the filming of one of the scenes in the film. Though it was not selected, the church remains a quaint structure that still stands. The church was then being used by a congregation of another denomination. It is now known as the Wesley Christian Church.

Wesley Methodist Church members: top row (l to r): Mayor William Seele, Edmund Edwards, Charles A. Seele, Jr., Samuel Keller; 2nd row: Mary Mack, Lucille Rowe, Earnestine Bennett, Theodosia Bryant, Mozelle Mack, Mildred Daniels; 3rd row: Helena Seele, Isabelle Seele, Mary Bowman, unidentified Minister, Gertrude Washington, Anna Edwards, Edna Seele; front row seated: Elizabeth Douglas, Lillie Mae Daniels, Mary L. Bennett, Samuel Bennett, Jr., unidentified child.

Mount Zion Baptist Church

In 1870, in an area located north of Lincolnville, the community of Dunmeyer was started. The first people to purchase land and settle there were the Joseph Dunmeyer family. Though the second family of settlers is unknown, Adonis Dezelle and his family were the third settlers to purchase land and move to this community. Adonis Dezelle told others about the many acres of land that were available in the area, and many people eager to purchase land moved to this community. It was later called Dunmeyer Hill.

Adonis Dezelle had a large grapevine on his property. He told others that it was revealed to him by God to build this grape arbor. He believed that God had a purpose for this arbor and that was for him to build a church.

In 1888 the first church, a wooden structure, was built. This church was given the name Mount Zion. It was furnished

Mount Zion Baptist Church

with a heater and lamp lights. The pastor was Anthony Alston; Adonis Dezelle was a deacon. The membership was made up of many members of the Morris Street Baptist Church in Charleston. The mother of the church was Phyliss Dezelle, wife of Adonis.

    Rev. A. M. Faulks pastored the church for a period of time. Rev. Lewis H. Simmons was the next to lead this congregation. During Reverend Simmons's term as pastor, the church was expanded. The next pastor to serve was Rev. Charles Bolgers. He led the congregation faithfully for many years. In the 1960s Reverend Faulks was called to serve a second term and during this time a second church was built and then destroyed by fire. The pastor and members of Philadelphia Baptist Church in Ladson opened their doors to Mount Zion members until they could rebuild their church. A third cinder-block structure was built at the original location. Rev. A. M. Faulks served this congregation until he died in 1969.

    Rev. Eddie Salley, Sr., was the next to serve as pastor; his son, Rev. Leon Salley, was the assistant pastor. During Rev. Salley's pastorate, there were many sorrow-filled times. Some of the members who died were: Henry Dezelle, Marie Dezelle, A. Brown, Della Dezelle, Mary Martin, and the mother of the church, Mattie Salley. There were also some joyful times, as much work helped improve the church. The church grew spiritually as the physical facility expanded. Pews were purchased in 1974, a dining area was added in 1977, and an air conditioner was purchased in 1983. In 1986 a pastor's study was added to the church and the seating area was extended. A mural by Floyd Gordon was painted on a wall inside the church. The graveyard area was maintained by W. E. Carpenter, Rev. Leon Salley, Adonis Dezelle and others.

    In 1987 the front of the church building was refaced with stone and a new roof was put on the church. Rev. Leon Salley was installed as pastor in 1992. Many children were rededicated to God. A central air and heating system, and a new steeple were purchased and installed. In 1995 two faithful members, Sara Bell Jones and Sarah Carpenter, were called to the great beyond. Land was purchased to extend the graveyard and parking area in 1995.

In 1996 a security system was installed in the church. The Missionary Board purchased table scarves and a communion table set.

    Mount Zion is blessed to celebrate 108 years of existence. Their motto: "Upon this Rock I build my church and the gates of hell shall not prevail against it."

Nazareth Holiness Church of Deliverance #2

The founding fathers of Nazareth Holiness Church of Deliverance #2 traveled many paths before finally settling in their present location. Determined to worship and serve God, they started meeting at the old Lincolnville Town Hall, then moved to the present Charles Ross Municipal Complex. The church was then known as Friendship Church of God in Christ. The membership decided to move to Aiken's Funeral Chapel in Summerville, and finally to a trailer on the present site on Carolina Street in Lincolnville, where the "Rose of Sharon Cathedral," Nazareth Holiness Church of Deliverance #2, was constructed.

The present bishop, Elder Jessie Jennings, accepted the charge of Friendship Church of God in Christ in Lincolnville in 1969, under Pastor Paul Taylor. The church at that time had only two adult members and some small children. The church became Nazareth Holiness Church of Deliverance #2 in 1978 under Bishop H. J. Jennings.

Nazareth Holiness Church of Deliverance #2

The church has gone through many trials, tribulations, and persecutions, but through God's grace they have come out victorious. During the construction of the church there were many problems—among other issues, the roof collapsed twice—but this dedicated group of people stayed consistent and persevered by fasting, praying, and by following their leader, Bishop Jennings.

Through this spirit-led ministry many have come to know God. The bishop regularly reminds the membership of these words from the book of Revelation 2:10: "Be thou faithful unto death and you shall receive a crown of life."

Friendship Inspirational Church of God in Christ

In 1966 Missionary Carolee Simmons opened her home on Railroad Avenue in Lincolnville for services each Sunday morning. The membership consisted of two missionaries and their children. When the membership grew, the services moved to the Lincolnville Town Hall. Services were held each Tuesday and Sunday. The officers at that time consisted of Missionaries Isabel Felder and Simmons. These ladies served as deacons, ushers, Sunday School teachers, and other positions as needed.

Shortly after moving to the Lincolnville Town Hall, Elder Paul Taylor, the district superintendent of the Church of God in Christ, served as pastor for one year.

During the 1968 Holy convocation, Elder Jessie Jennings, Jr., was appointed pastor of the church, which was now called Friendship. He served in that capacity for 12 years. The

Friendship Inspirational Church of God in Christ

first deacon of Friendship was the late Gamerlear Williams. The membership then consisted of members of the Felder, Simmons, Simpson, and Williams families. About that time, .66 acres of land were purchased at the corner of Front and Hamilton streets. The foundation was laid and the block structure of the Friendship Church of God in Christ was erected.

In 1979 Elder Johnnie J. Johnson was appointed interim pastor. Elder Johnson served for one year. During his service, the roof was placed on the building.

In November 1980 Elder Edward L. Johnson, along with the members of Friendship moved from Lincolnville Town Hall to the kitchen area of the church. In 1981 Elder Johnson was appointed pastor of the church. Through prayer, fasting, rallies, and other fundraisers, the members of Friendship were able to build a new sanctuary and move into it in October 1984.

Because Elder Johnson was always inspired by the Lord, the Friendship Church of God in Christ became known as the Friendship Inspirational Church of God in Christ. Through continued fasting and prayer and under the leadership of Pastor Johnson, the sanctuary was completed. Friendship has continued to grow in every way.

Pastor Johnson and the members at Friendship have been blessed to acquire central heating and air systems and a paved parking lot. They have installed comfortable seating and carpeting. The members purchased an additional acre of land where they have built their new Family Life Center.

Lydia Baptist Church

Lydia Baptist Church is located on Owens Drive near the Lincolnville Town limit. Many residents attend this church.

Lincolnville Police Department

To protect the safety of Lincolnville citizens, in the first years after its founding the town leaders developed laws and before long hired a marshal.

The earliest city record that identifies a town officer shows that Marshal Wilson was given the job of protecting the town in May 1920. The intendant (mayor) at that time was Charles Augustus Seele.

A small jail was built on Smith Street to hold those charged with minor crimes. More serious offenders were taken to the Charleston County lock-up. The Lincolnville jail was temporarily closed by the county health department in 1933 because it did not meet health standards. The jail is still in existence as an historical reminder of the past. After the closing of the jail, all prisoners were transported to the Charleston County jail.

Marshal Joseph Manley, circa 1945

Through the years, many men have served as marshal. The next marshal on record was Joseph "Joe" Manley. There was always a great turnover rate in the police department due to the low salary. As a result, Lincolnville was occasionally without a police officer. During those times, Charleston County sheriff deputies patrolled the town. During the early 1950s

Marshal George Gardner served as the one-man police force. His wife Mary Gardner prepared and delivered meals to the prisoners. She also cleaned the jail linens. George Gardner served as marshal until 1953. Following his tenure, George White protected the town for a short period of time before Marshal Sam Bennett took over the job in 1954. He served until 1969.

The town purchased its first police cruiser in 1969 for $585. Mayor Charles Ross acquired the two-door 1965 unmarked Highway Department car. The cruiser was sent to Charleston for the installation of a two-way radio which was tied into the Charleston County police network. The department continued improving, and in 1969 Charles Bell, the first riding policeman, was hired.

Lincolnville's old jail

On May 1, 1982, Mayor Charles Ross sought additional help in improving the town's law enforcement from U.S. Senator Strom Thurmond. Town records suggest that the funding was not received, as the town had to take out a loan to purchase a new police car.

In August 1983 the 911 system was brought to the town.

The citizens of Lincolnville assisted the police department in protecting the town by forming a Crime Watch orga-

Officer Kenneth Vann and Mayor Charles

nization in 1992, with Enoch Dickerson serving as president. Other members were Hattie Salley, Helen Anderson, Dorothy Bailey, Alice Smith, Laverne Williams, and James C. Hampton. Each year the Crime Watch committee recognized the town's honor roll students by distributing awards and money. They also recognized high school and college graduates.

They sponsored a Valentine tea and May Day celebration. They also provided Thanksgiving baskets, put on back-to-school parties, and sponsored a bus trip to James Island County Park to see the Christmas lights.

Judge Enoch Dickerson and Helen Anderson, Miss Crime Watch.

Officer Richard Hill (center) and fellow constables

The Civic League joined the police department in sponsoring Law Enforcement Day for the citizens of the town. These events have featured the City of Charleston's horse patrol, a helicopter, one of the city's sporty Camaros, and other popular attractions. Each year the police department participates in the Fourth of July parade and helps with the Christmas celebration.

On April 2003 the town passed a resolution to utilize the services of the South Carolina State Constable Program. In January 2004 a new Public Safety Building was dedicated which allowed the police and fire departments to share the same modern facilities.

At different times, Councilmen Charles Duberry and James C. Hampton have served as council members in charge of the Public Safety Department. Hampton currently holds the title of Pubic Safety director.

Lincolnville Police Officer Kenneth Vann invites City of Charleston and Charleston County Police Department to participate in Law Enforcement Day sponsored by the Civic League.

Partial List of Law Enforcement Officers

Marshal Wilson	1920
Joseph Manley	
George Gardner	
George White	July 1953
Sam Bennett	August 1954 - July 1969
Charles Bell	
James Cakely	
Nathaniel Hardee	July 1970
James Thomas	June 1973
Russ Cooper	1973
James Pasley	
Leroy Meyers	January 1974
Leo Pavlovich	1977
David Sharp	1979-1980
Officer Stillwell	1982
Officer Platt	
Officer Crosby	1983
Donnie White	
Iris Walker	
Leo Snyder	
Officer Howard	
Officer Frazier	
Officer Trammell	1986
Joseph Schneider	1986-1992
Officer Shivers	
Eric Bradley	
Officer Wolf	1992
Kenneth Vann	1993-2000
Eric Bradley	2000
Richard Hill	2000-Present

86

Lincolnville Volunteer Fire Department

The earliest Lincolnville settlers realized that they needed to organize the citizens to deal with disasters or other safety issues in the town. They came together to protect the health and safety of the entire town. Until the late 1960s every man in town served as a firefighter. The town also relied on mutual aid from surrounding fire departments.

In 1968 Mayor Charles Ross contracted to use a small fire truck that belonged to a group located in Ladson, South Carolina.

Lincolnville Volunteer Firemen prepare for the 4th of July parade, 1991.

The truck was parked at a service station on U. S. Highway 78, a central location for both communities.

In 1969 the City of Charleston gave the town a bigger truck, a 1942 Chevrolet which carried 400 gallons of water. Charleston's fire chief Wilmot Guthke presented the truck to Mayor Ross. The firemen from Charleston also trained the Lincolnville firemen in the truck's operation. This truck was parked under a live oak tree next to a Lincolnville store owned by Leon Miller, Sr., who became the first fire chief. Other charter members of the Fire Department were Arnic J. Washington (who served from 1968 until 1998), Leon Miller, Jr., Fred Noble, Sr., George Jacobs, Miller Ross, Samuel Keller, John Douglas, and Richard Drayton. The next truck was also donated to the town. Mayor Ross and the town's policeman, Russ Cooper, drove to Maryland to pick up a truck after arrangements had been made by U.S. Senator Strom Thurmond.

The first fire station was built in 1979 when the General Electric Company in Ladson donated an old house. The Lincoln-

The Old Lincolnville Fire Department (left) and the New Public Safety Building (below).

ville firemen dismantled it by hand and rebuilt it on Smith Street next to the old jail. That station was designed by Clay Aiken, Sr. Its cornerstone includes the following information:

> Mayor: Charles Ross
> Council: George Jacobs
>   Harold Douglas
>   Arnic J. Washington
>   Samuel Cox, Sr.
>   Willie Brown (deceased)
> Volunteer Firemen: Gamerlear Williams (Chief)
>   T. Sellers Sr.
>   W. M. Montgomery, Jr.
>   J. H. Miller
>   R. Drayton
>   L. A. Daniel
>   C. Campbell, Sr.
>   D. Fiddie
>   L. A. Goode
>   C. Gleaton
> Clerk Treasurer: C. Duberry, Jr.
> Attorney: Bernard R. Fielding
> Assessor Chairman: John J. Douglas
> Secretary: Mildred Cox
>   Josh Bell
> Founder Fire Department: Harold W. Bennett
> Designer: Clay Aiken, Sr.

The Fire Department volunteers continued working to protect the community, but were in a constant struggle to keep their truck up and running. They searched for equipment from departments in surrounding communities that could be donated to the town.

In 1979 James C. Hampton became fire chief. He acquired more equipment for the department and oversaw the installation of an alert system. The department grew and more people volun-

Captain Arnic J. Washington, a lifetime volunteer fireman, served Lincolnville for six years as mayor pro tem, 18 years as councilman, and 30 years as an active volunteer fireman (1968-1998).

teered. Because of the modernization of the Fire Department, the town's insurance ratings improved and the rates for Lincolnville citizens were lowered. In 1982 the town passed a tax hike to pay for its first new truck. Vehicles have been donated from other communities: About 1996 the department received a truck from a town in New Jersey and in 1999 the town received a Mack fire truck from North Charleston.

Like the Police Department, the Fire Department is actively involved in projects to benefit the community. Chiefs, volunteers, and junior cadets have participated in the March of Dimes drives, collecting funds to help sick children. They have sponsored New Year's Eve dances and Pre-Valentine dances. At Halloween they also sponsor the Trick or Treat event and Haunted

House. They participate in parades in Summerville, Charleston Air Force Base, Sullivan's Island, and many other communities. With the Civic League the deparment sponsors the Christmas tree lighting celebration.

In January 2004 the new Public Safety Facility was dedicated. The Fire Department continues in the new facility with the following staff:

    Public Safety Director: James C. Hampton, Councilman
    Fire Chief: Charles Gantt
    Paid Fireman: Edward Simpson
    Volunteers: Rick Boyd, Patrick Clyde, Michael Hicks, Blair McDowell, Joe Pedalino, Clark Presley, Steven Roberts, Bobby Robinson, Edward Simpson, Ed Skiba, and Bo Williams.

Through the years, some of the men and women who have served in the development of the Fire Department are:

Fire Chiefs: Leon Miller, Harold W. Bennett, John Douglas, Gamerlear Williams, James C. Hampton, J.B. Wagoner, Tom Irvin, Steven Roberts, Leland Shannon, Robert Roberson, John Hendricks, and Charles Gantt;

Christmas Tree Lighting Ceremony.
(l to r): Fire Chief Charles Gantt, Officer Richard Hill, Mayor Tyrone Aiken, and Coucilman James C. Hampton.

Volunteers: Edward Aiken, Clyde Bland, Rick Boyd, Clarence Campbell, Patrick Clyde, Samuel Cox, Leroy Daniels, Harold Douglas, Richard Drayton, Charles Duberry, D. Fiddie, Charles Gleaton, Lloyd A. Goode, Kevin Haynes, Michael Hicks, Karl Hofen, Harold Huger, George Jacobs, Marshall Kelly, Blair McDowell, J. H. Miller, Mr. Mincey, William Montgomery, Jr., Joe Pedalino, Clark Presley, Albert Roberts, D. K. Roberts, Steven Roberts, Bobby Robinson, Joyce Sanders, Theodore Sellers, Leland Shannon, Edward Simpson (who began work with the Fire Department as a volunteer and later served as the only paid fireman for many years), Ed Skiba, Thomas Walden, Arnic J. Washington, Bo Williams, and Sam Williams; and

Junior Cadets: Jamie Carn, Jay Craven, Kenny Craven, Michael Craven, Mike Crocker, Gordon Hill Jr., Eric Sellers, and Dennis Weaver.

In 1993 the Fire Department honored Lorraine Huger (r) as Miss Flame, while Sherri Aiken (l) was recognized as Miss Lincolnville.

Civic League

In 1944 a group of concerned ladies headed by Louise Hill, who resided in Lincolnville at the time, became interested in the civic affairs of the town. These ladies formed an organization known as The Cosmopolitan Civic League (later shortened to Civic League). They started out with absolutely nothing as far as finances were concerned. But they had great ideas, and these ideas were exercised in the form of work.

They began by having parties for the youth of the community every Friday night. It was a delightful idea for the young people because they were desperate for some form of decent recreation. Youth as far away as Charleston came by bus to attend picnics in Lincolnville.

Louise Hill, founder of the Civic League, with her husband David Seabrook Hill.

The Civic League sponsored programs that were educational for all citizens of the town. The first Piccolo (juke box) for the Town Hall was purchased by the ladies of the Civic League. They also purchased playground equipment and placed

it on the Town Hall property, which was then located at the Williams Graded School.

As time passed, some of the ladies moved away and others died, but the faithful few carried on. They worked under some very hard con-

The Civic League worked with the town to erect the first welcome sign (above).

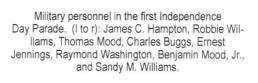

Military personnel in the first Independence Day Parade. (l to r): James C. Hampton, Robbie Williams, Thomas Mood, Charles Buggs, Ernest Jennings, Raymond Washington, Benjamin Mood, Jr., and Sandy M. Williams.

Myra A. Washington representing Lincolnville in the Miss Black Teenage South Carolina Beauty Pageant in Charleston, 1973.

ditions. Among the accomplishments made over the years by the Civic League are: installing a fence around the play area at the original Town Hall; repairing the Town Hall furnace; plumbing the Town Hall bathroom and kitchen; purchasing a piano, tables and chairs, microphone, and a Leland Cypress tree. The tree is decorated each year for the Christmas tree lighting celebration. The celebration was one of the many programs started by the Civic League. The League brought much recognition and improvement to the town when the ladies purchased and erected two "Welcome to Lincolnville" signs.

At the present time, the group is small in number but continues to work for the enhancement of the town. The members organized the Independence Day parade in 1991 under Mayor Zelma Fielding's administration. All branches of the military participated in the parade. Special recognition was given to the two returning heroes from Operation Desert Storm, First Sgt. Sandy M. Williams and Staff Sgt. Ernest Jennings. Miss Lincolnville, Denise RaeShawn Gleaton, was a beautiful representative of the community. The Civic League sponsored the parade until a new administration appointed a separate organization to sponsor the parade.

The Civic League was instrumental in restarting the Summer Lunch Program for the children of the community. This was done under the leadership of Rosalee Williams Washington, a dedicated member. The group also sponsored educational activities for the children during their summer vacations. The summer program included such activities as swimming safety, storytelling, demonstrations on safety from the Police Department, crafts, and games. A fashion show was put on for senior citizens. The Civic League also sponsored a Community Spring Tea for many years. The group has given financial and moral support to families in the community in times of distress, such as deaths, illnesses, or fires. In 2001 the Civic League began a Quilting Club for all ages.

left: Miss Lincolnville 1991 Denise RaeShawn Gleaton;
right: Miss Lincolnville 1984 Michelle Gleaton.

Rev. Anna Rebecca Williams, one of the surviving charter members of the Civic League.

The Civic League applied for and was awarded a grant through the Coastal Community Foundation to help with its beautification project. Through this grant the members purchased the "Yard of the Month" sign and a motivational sign. The motivational sign is a symbol showing characters representing "Anti-Litter and Uncle Pride," which stands for "All Lincolnvillians United with Pride."

The surviving charter member living in Lincolnville is Rev. Anna Rebecca Williams. The other surviving charter member is Louise Hill, now of Charleston.

The deceased charter members are: Wilhemenia Barron, Mary Bowman, Florence Craig, Janie Douglas, Anna Edwards, Hattie Frazier, Albertha Jacobs, Earnestine Mance, Rachel McCray, Ida Ross, Edna Seele, Isabelle Seele and Gertrude Washington.

Much of the history of this organization came from the notes that Ida Ross kept for the group.

Among the past presidents who helped guide the League are: Louise Hill, Florence

The Yard of the Month sign features Uncle Pride and Anti-Litter.

Craig, Gertrude Washington, Ruth Ross, Rosalee W. Washington, and Barbara Dease. The current president is Christine Williams Hampton who has served from 1979 to the present.

Some of the current and past members are:

Bernice Aiken	Albertha Jacobs
Stella Aiken	Elise Johnson
Dorothy Bailey	Georgia Kelly
Wilhemenia Barron	Gladys Lincoln
Ollie Blake	Bessie Linen
Mary Bowman	Earnestine Mance
Odessa Bowman	Rachel McCray
Bernesta Campbell	Albertha Montgomery
Sarah Carpenter	Lucille Noble
Rev. Mildred Cox	Ida Ross
Florence Craig	Ruth Ross
Eartha Lee Daniels	Dorothy Salley
Barbara Dease	Hattie Mae Salley
Annette Douglas	Mattie Salley
Elaine Douglas	Edna Seele
Janie Douglas	Carrie Sellers
Eloise Duberry	Lottie Singleton
Lorraine Duberry	Alice Smith
Anna Edwards	Inez Turner
Hattie Frazier	Gertrude Washington
Rev. Anna R. Williams Gleaton	Rosalee W. Washington
	Rev. Anna Rebecca Williams
Dorothy Glover	Annabelle Williams
Christine W. Hampton	Laverne Williams
Louise Hill	Mary Williams
Laura Iricks	

The Health Department and Civic League sponsored the Health Fair.
Pictured (l to r): Rosalee W. Washington, Tonya Haynes, Anna Ruth Gleaton (sponsor), Officer Eric Bradley, Fire Chief Charles Gantt, Mayor Tyrone Aiken, Dr. Quincy, Alice W. Smith, Christine W. Hampton.

Highlighting Citizens

Lincolnville is proud of all its citizens, those of the past and the present. Some of Lincolnville's leading citizens not presented in other chapters are featured in this chapter.

Wilhemenia Alston Barron

Wilhemenia Alston Barron was a descendant of one of the early families that settled in Lincolnville. It is not known where she received her early education, but she graduated from South Carolina State College with a Bachelor's Degree in Education. After the second world war, she taught in Berkeley County and then in Charleston County for many years. Later, she assumed the dual role of teacher and principal of Lincolnville Elementary School.

Her grandmother, who lived on Meeting Street in Lincolnville, raised her. In later years, she met and married Daniel Ben Barron. They lived in a beautiful home on Dunmeyer Hill Road in Lincolnville. They were the only family in town with a fishpond in the yard. The children of the community loved to visit the Barrons to see the beautiful goldfish.

Wilhemenia Barron loved children. This was evident in her work with them in the public schools and at the Ebenezer A.M.E. Church Sunday School. She served as a Sunday School teacher and, after the death of her husband, superintendent. She was an active member of Ebenezer. She loved singing with the senior choir.

She was affiliated with the Order of the Eastern Stars (New Eden Chapter) in Summerville, the American Association of University Women, and the Alpha Gamma Chi sorority.

James Christopher Hampton

James Christopher Hampton was born in Charleston, South Carolina. He lived in Lincolnville and moved away after graduating from college. He is the son of James and Christine W. Hampton.

James attended Ladson Elementary School, Alice Birney Middle School, and R.B. Stall High School, where he was enrolled in the Gifted and Talented academic programs. During his senior year in high school, James was presented in the Beuax Affair Progam for young men, a leadership program presented by Charleston Youth Leadership Council, Inc. He received a college scholarship from the program. James also received $40,000 in college scholarships from Florida A&M University and South Carolina State University.

While at R.B. Stall, he received the Phi Beta Sigma Fraterntiy Excellence Award. He participated as a member of the Stall football team for five years. He attended the Georgia Tech Minority Introduction to Engineering Program during the summer of 1993. He also was a member of Stall High School's state championship Bicentennial Team. This team traveled to Washington, D.C., to compete against teams from the other 49 states and the District of Columbia. While living in Lincolnville, he attended Ebenezer A.M.E. Church

James has always loved airplanes and grew up wanting to be a fighter pilot. He also loved science, and as a child was curious about how things worked. That curiosity led to his obtaining a Bachelor's Degree in Electrical Engineering Technology from South Carolina State University. While at S.C. State, he joined the Alpha Phi Alpha fraternity where he was a regular volunteer at a senior citizen home. He worked each summer in the engineering field, such as a summer mentoring program for incoming engineering majors. He also served internships at the Savannah River Plant in Augusta, Ga., and the Veterans Administration Hospital in Charleston. James is currently enrolled in the Master's Degree Program at the Keller Graduate School of Business in Atlanta. His love for aircrafts helped him gain the position of systems engineer at Lockheed Martin Aeronautics Company in Marietta, Ga.

James is currently vice president of Market Street Investments, LLC, an investment firm that he and several of his childhood friends created. He has also started his own company, Hampton Development and Consulting, through which he focuses on real estate development. These companies are located in the Atlanta area.

David Seabrook Hill

David Seabrook Hill was the son of Mattie Seabrook Hill, the first teacher of the Williams Graded School, and David R. Hill, also a schoolteacher. David moved to Charleston as a young boy, and attended segregated schools. Later he attended a boarding school in Orangeburg, which is now South Carolina State University. In 1919, at the age of 17, David began work as a shipwright apprentice for 75 cents an hour or $6.00 a day. David worked at the Charleston Naval Shipyard for 30 years. He retired in 1962.

David Seabrook Hill was very active in Charleston politics. At the age of 91 he led a petition drive with a goal to "Save the Shipyard."

David was married to Louise Hill, who helped organize Lincolnville's Civic League. David and Louise lived in Lincolnville for a short time as a young married couple before moving back to Charleston. They are the parents of two children, Harold and Carol, and five grandchildren.

Mattie Seabrook Hill (seated front row) with her children, including her son David Seabrook Hill (standing, second from right).

Alonzo William Holman

Alonzo William Holman, son of the late Alonzo F. and Lillie Bell Ross Holman, was a native of Lincolnville. A member of the A.M.E. church his entire life, Reverend Holman dedicated his life's work to serving others.

Reverend Holman was a product of Lincolnville Elementary School, Burke High School in Charleston, Allen University, and Dickerson Theological Seminary, both in Columbia, South Carolina. Allen honored him with a Doctor of Divinity Degree in 1975. The next year Edward Waters College of Jacksonville, Florida, did the same, and Monrovia College in Liberia, West Africa, bestowed his third Doctor of Divinity Degree in 1988.

Called at an early age, he began preaching at 16 in 1951. He was ordained both an itinerant deacon and elder in 1953.

For more than 43 years, he was blessed to share marriage with the former Gerald E. Smith of Anderson, South Carolina.

He pastored the Waterloo Circuit in Laurens County, South Carolina; Graniteville Circuit in Graniteville, South Carolina; for ten years Cumberland A.M.E. Church in Aiken, South Carolina; and for ten more years "Mother Emanuel" A.M.E. Church, Charleston.

While serving as pastor of Emanuel A.M.E. he was elected a general officer in the A.M.E. Church in July 1988 and served as the director of salary supplement of the church, headquartered in Memphis, Tennessee. After twelve years of service, he retired in 2000. He served in the active ministry for 50 years.

Reverend Holman served as secretary of the Board of Trustees of Allen University, was a member of the General Board of the A.M.E. Church, secretary of the Commission on Statistics and Finance, and secretary of the Subcommittee of Budget. He served as an officer of the Episcopal Committee for four quadrennials. He was a member of every General Conference since 1964. He was elected president of the Pastors Council of the Seventh Episcopal District and represented the A.M.E. Church on the Commission on Faith and Order of the National Council of Churches, USA. He served as a member of the Commission of Stewardship of the National Council of Churches, USA. He was president of the General Officers' Council of the A.M.E. Church.

He was a member of the Board of Directors of the Ecumenical Center for Stewardship Studies, and served there on the Executive Committee, Forums of Theological Studies, and the Planning Committee on the North American Conference on Christian Philanthropy. The ECSS represents 29 denominations in the USA and Canada. He served a five-year term on the Board of Directors of the World Methodist Council.

Reverend Holman dedicated much of his life to civic activities. He served with distinction for 19 years on the Board of the South Carolina Department of Youth Service, including four separate terms as chairman. He was state president of the NAACP, and served seven years on the organization's national Board of Directors. During that period, at the 1968 National Convention of the NAACP, he served as chairman of two standing committees, Advanced Drafting and Time and Place. He participated in three White House Conferences, was consultant to the U.S. Equal Employment Opportunity Commission, and served on the United States Selective Services Appeals Board and the Committee on Hunger and Malnutrition in South Carolina. He was a delegate to the 1968 National Democratic Convention, serving as co-vice-chairman of the South Carolina delegation.

Governor Carroll Campbell appointed him to an at-large seat on the South Carolina Alcohol and Drug Board. He resigned this position when he was elected a General Officer of his church.

Reverend Holman has been listed in *Who's Who in American Politics* and *Who's Who among Black Clergymen*. He was a member of Effingham Lodge K#98 of Prince Hall Free and Accepted Masons. The South Carolina Youth Workers Association for 1987 presented him the Distinguished Service Award. He was an Honorary Kentucky Colonel and an Honorary Tennessee Colonel. Upon leaving Charleston, the City of Charleston declared August 26, 1988, as Reverend Alonzo W. Holman Day. Governor Richard Riley awarded him the Order of Palmetto, the highest honor bestowed on a South Carolina citizen.

Dr. Lawrence James

Dr. Lawrence James is the son of Azalee James and the late Isaac James. He is the brother of Louis James, the late Robert James, and the late Leroy James. His sisters are Christine Moses and Gloria Dezelle.

Lawrence attended Lincolnville Elementary School, where he excelled in academics. He also represented the school and won recognition and awards in the Charleston County District Oratorical Speaking Contests for several years. Lawrence graduated as salutatorian from Lincolnville Elementary in 1962. He then attended Bonds-Wilson High School in North Charleston, where he graduated as valedictorian in 1967. Four years later, in 1971, he graduated with a Bachelor's Degree in Chemistry and minor in Drama from South Carolina State University. While at SCSU, Lawrence became a member of the famous Henderson-Davis Players dramatic group, with whom he performed many roles, won many awards for the university, and toured in England and Scotland in the summer of 1971 as a part of the American Theatre Festival in Europe.

Lawrence then attended Texas Tech University and received the Master of Arts degree in Theatre in 1972. From there he entered the doctoral program as a graduate teaching assistant at Wayne State University, Detroit, where he received the Doctor of Philosophy degree in Speech Communications and Theatre in 1976. Lawrence served as director of Black Theatre at Illinois State University, 1975-76, and then returned to Wayne State as assistant professor, 1976-80. Lawrence moved to Tennessee and became part of the faculty of Tennessee State University in 1980.

At Tennessee State, Dr. James serves as professor of theatre, has directed many productions, and is a member of the Honors faculty. Dr. James heads the Department of Communications, one of the largest departments at the university, with discipline areas in Speech Communications, Mass Communications, and Theatre.

An important part of Lawrence's career has been his work as director of Worship Arts at Born Again Church, overseeing a ministry of dramatic and dance arts which has traveled nationally and internationally, spreading the gospel of Jesus Christ. Dr. James's career spans the realms of teacher, administrator, artistic director, consultant, and religious-arts specialist.

Lawrence is married to Eleanor Franklin James, of Detroit, Michigan. They have three children, Christopher, Evan, and Lauren. They reside in Nashville, Tennessee.

Lawrence gives all glory and honor to God for all his blessings, gifts, and talents, the opportunities for travel, and his many career accomplishments. Lawrence sees his greatest accomplishments as being a godly husband, father, and minister of Christ. "To God be the Glory!"

He notes, "I know in great part I have been blessed by having a great family foundation, with many sacrifices for my education, while teaching me the important foundations of love, discipline, hard work, and respect. Moreover, I learned much from my teachers (e.g., Mrs. Carrie Lou Aiken, Mrs. Wilhemenia Alston Barron, and many others, including Mrs. Mack of Bonds-Wilson), mentors (e.g., the late Mayor Charles Ross), and the people of Lincolnville and Dunmeyer Hill, South Carolina, my home!"

John Henry McCray

John Henry McCray was born near Youngstown, Florida, on August 25, 1910. His family moved from Youngstown to Charleston, the birthplace of his mother, Rachel. The family later moved to Lincolnville. He attended Lincolnville Elementary School and the Avery Institute in Charleston. He received a degree from Talladega College in Alabama.

McCray is one of the most important black journalists in the history of South Carolina and was a towering figure during the civil-rights movement of the 1940s and 1950s.

In one of his articles from the *Charleston Chronicle*'s archives, he described his life growing up in Lincolnville: "we lived just across the tracks from the pump house that Mac Bradford operated for Southern Railroad during my growing up years." He remembered that "the water tank was nearby and we wild-eyed youngsters got chances to chat with the white engineers and Negro firemen when trains stopped to refuel."

Upon leaving college, he worked as the city editor of the *Charleston Messenger*, which was owned by the Jenkins Orphanage. He was able to run some good stories in the *Messenger*, but the management didn't want certain articles published. In 1938 he began producing a newspaper of his own, a weekly called the *Charleston Lighthouse*. After he moved to Columbia it was simply called *The Lighthouse*. In 1940 he combined that newspaper with the *People's Informer* of Sumter, South Carolina. *The Lighthouse and Informer* was published in Columbia until 1964.

In an interview, McCray stated that his "reason for going into the business, was to try to take up the cause of a people he felt had little coverage in the daily newspapers at that time other than crime. There were no Negro newspapers in that community at that time."

John Henry McCray had a multifaceted career. In addition to the titles of writer, editor, and publisher, he worked as a photographer in Columbia. He was also in great demand as a speaker and civil-rights activist.

Rachel McCray. Photographed by her son, John Henry McCray

In 1944 McCray was elected state chairman of the Progressive Democratic Party, and initiated a state-wide voter registration campaign. He was the chairman of a delegation to the national Democratic Convention in Chicago, which challenged the all-white South Carolina delegation. The national party voted to stand by the whites. As editor of *The Lighthouse and Informer*, he generated support for the NAACP's successful efforts to equalize black and white teacher salaries and to integrate the public schools.

Richard A. Ready

Richard A. Ready was a dynamic man who lived on Smith Street in Lincolnville. He lived in a large, two-story home with a beautiful wrap-around porch. His home was directly in front of Mary Bowman's Grocery Store. He is remembered as always being well groomed and owning a beautiful station wagon with wood panels on the sides.

R. A. Ready was an educator and musician. Professor Ready, as he was called, once served as organist of Bethel A.M.E. Church in Summerville. He also was pianist, assistant superintendent, and music director at Ebenezer A.M.E. Church Sunday School when William Washington was the superintendent.

Professor Ready served as a town warden when Charles Augustus Seele was mayor in 1920. He served on Town Council for many years. He later moved to Moncks Corner, where he built and operated a boarding house for teachers on the main street. Ready traveled back and forth between Moncks Corner and Lincolnville.

Richard Ready worked as an educator in Moncks Corner for many years. In 1920 he started teaching at Dixie Training, a "Rosenwald School." (Julius Rosenwald, the founder of Sears Roebuck, contributed millions of dollars for the construction of schools in the rural South for black children. Dixie Training was the first to receive such a grant in Berkeley County.) When R. A. Ready came to the three-room building, the school was staffed by three local people, including Lurlie Shine Heyward. In the fall of 1920 Mr. Ready worked with Ella Forrest and Wilhemenia Alston.

In 1921 R. A. Ready, Martha A. Toomer, Ella Forrest, and Norma Lee Johnson made up the staff.

Between 1920 and 1932 many teachers came and left the school but R. A. Ready and Ms. Toomer were fixtures there. Many of the teachers in the first years came from the Avery Institute in Charleston. Within five years of Professor Ready's arrival, the Manual Training Building was added. The boys and girls did specialized work there. Some of the teachers who worked with Professor Ready were Anita Cole, Frank Gadsden, Naomi Bacote, Alma Latten, Ruth M. Myers, L. H. Lindsey, Earnest E. Everett, and Mildred Wigfall.

At some point the name of the school was changed from Dixie Training to R. A. Ready Elementary, before it was finally changed after integration to Berkeley Middle School.

Richard A. Ready touched the lives of many African-American children who lived in Moncks Corner. He died in 1952 and according to some who attended his funeral he is buried in Bible Sojourn Cemetery in Lincolnville.

Charlotte S. Riley

Charlotte S. Riley was born August 26, 1839, of poor slave parents in Charleston. She was their only girl, and reportedly displayed a spirit superior to those of her four brothers.

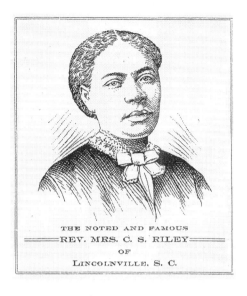

THE NOTED AND FAMOUS REV. MRS. C. S. RILEY OF LINCOLNVILLE, S. C.

Southern state laws then were very rigid against slaves being taught to read and write. The children were allowed to attend trade schools that would help them provide a profit for their owners. When Charlotte attended trade school, the teachers also taught her and her fellow students to recite their lessons.

As a child, Charlotte experienced poor health, suffering nervous headaches. And yet despite the pain, she retained what she was taught. The condition led Charlotte to the title of her autobiography, *A Mysterious Life and Calling*. She claimed that at the age of fourteen she was mysteriously converted to the religion of the Lord Jesus at an old-time Methodist watch night meeting on Sullivan's Island.

After Charlotte's conversion, she joined a Presbyterian Church. Her father, John Levy, and her grandmother raised her. After her father died in 1861, Charlotte's grandmother raised her and her brothers.

During the Civil War, Charlotte left Charleston, refugeeing to Anderson with her mistress, Mrs. John Wilkes, who Charlotte called her "mother." While in Anderson, she met and eventually married Cornelius Riley.

After the war, Cornelius and Charlotte moved from Anderson and settled in Columbia, South Carolina. They later moved back to her birthplace, Charleston.

There were many calls for Charlotte's services as an educator. She accepted a position at a Presbyterian school near Charleston. She also taught a night school for young men and women who could not attend day school. Her husband did not like Charleston and, against Charlotte's wishes, moved back to Columbia.

A request for her services came from Richard Harvey Cain, presiding A.M.E. elder for the Orangeburg District, and other church leaders for Charlotte to work for her people. They hoped she would teach in a new school, to be opened in October 1867 in the town of Lewisville (now St. Matthews), South Carolina. She agreed in principle, but waited for her husband to return from Columbia before she gave her final answer.

When she first met Bishop Cain, he questioned her about her religious affiliation. Upon hearing that she was Presbyterian, the bishop convinced her that as a woman of great gifts she should leave her home church. To test her commitment, he asked her to help raise funds. She consented to put on a sacred tableau program for two nights and raised $118.00, using only $18.00 for expenses. She accepted the lesson taught as this: "To accomplish the greater good, one must go where she is most needed."

She started in Lewisville with 25 children. When she complained about her boarding place, the church elders built her a house near the school. However, Charlotte's husband later changed his mind about letting her teach in Lewisville. He said, "I don't want you around those African Methodist." Charlotte told him that her word was her bond, and he gave up the verbal battle, though he threatened "never to come to see her." Charlotte stated, "The battle was fought, the victory won, and Zion's field is mine's."

Charlotte taught adults at night and children during the day for six months, five hours a day. With the help of two other teachers, she also taught Sabbath School to 300 men, women, and children. Eventually, the day school came under the control of the state. Charlotte then received back pay of $1,300 for her three years service teaching students whose parents could not pay. Charlotte also taught sharecroppers how to become self-sufficient.

Charlotte did much work as a traveling local missionary. During her travels, both whites and Negroes came to see and hear her. After many years of religious travel, her physician advised her to move to another area for a rest. She had previously purchased a pretty little home in Lincolnville, so Charlotte went there.

After Charlotte regained her strength, she traveled to New York and New Jersey. While in Patterson, New Jersey, she encountered the Rev. Henry Matthews, who invited her to visit his church. Though he asked if she would preach, her weakness prevented her from doing so. But when pressed to give words of encouragement, she chided the members of the congregation for not having their own house of worship. She later remembered telling them, "We down South were worshipping in our own house, but if the white man shall say to you tomorrow, 'Come out of my school house,' where will you go?" That very night the church members began to collect money for a building of their own, which they eventually built.

On August 20, 1885, Charlotte was appointed postmistress for the town of Lincolnville. The former postmistress, Catherine Wallace, recommended her for the job. Her adopted son David Riley Hill assisted her in the work.

In 1902 Charlotte wrote to President Theodore Roosevelt requesting that he have his train slow down as he passed through Lincolnville so the people could see their president. As the president's train approached Lincolnville, President Roosevelt appeared on the rear platform with his aide and doffed his handsome silk beaver hat to the assembled crowd.

Charlotte was always involved in community activities in Lincolnville. She was known for her generous hospitality. Sidney Woodward, a noted opera singer, resided with her when he performed in Summerville.

Charlotte organized an Educational Association in Lincolnville, and served as treasurer. Some of the other officers were also noted early settlers: William H. Washington, a former mayor, president; Rev. Marc Buffet, vice president; and Mattie Seabrook, secretary.

Charlotte also actively supported the Scott's Industrial School located in Ladson and the Orphan Industrial Farm (later known as Rev. Daniel Jenkins's Orphanage) as a manager. Other managers of the farm were: Rev. Daniel J. Jenkins, Professor F. W. Hoffman, Dr. William D. Crum, W. H. Johnson, Rev. J. A. Seal, E. R. Ayers, and William H. Washington.

Several clippings covering outstanding addresses made by Rev. C. S. Riley describe her as being one of the greatest female powers in society and the only woman preacher in the state.

The Rev. Mrs. Riley organized a Christian Educational Society in Lincolnville, which has helped the town develop. The membership grew rapidly each year.

Mrs. Riley's home was on an acre of land, nicely cultivated. Her flower garden with its numerous shrubs, roses, and other flowers was the pride of her heart. She called her flowers God's messengers of love.

Her doors were always open to strangers, as well as to friends, and all were made happy under her hospitable domain.

Pernessa C. Seele

Pernessa C. Seele is the daughter of Charles and Luella Seele. She was raised in Lincolnville, attended Lincolnville Elementary School, and graduated from R. B. Stall High School in North Charleston. She received a Master of Science Degree from Clark Atlanta University.

Ms. Seele is the founder and chief executive officer of The Balm in Gilead, a non-profit, non-government organization with an international mission to stop the spread of HIV/AIDS throughout the African diaspora. The Balm in Gilead is now the largest AIDS-awareness program in the United States targeting the African-American faith community. The group builds the capacity of faith communities to provide services, shares HIV/AIDS educational materials, and builds support networks for all people living with and affected by HIV/AIDS.

The Balm in Gilead's pioneering achievements have enabled thousands of churches both in the U.S. and throughout Africa to become leaders in preventing the transmission of HIV by providing comprehensive educational programs and offering compassionate support to all persons affected by HIV/AIDS.

Ms. Seele is one of the nation's most prominent voices on issues of HIV/AIDS and its effect on African people throughout the world. The Balm in Gilead is currently mobilizing faith communities in Côte d'Ivoire, Kenya, Nigeria, Tanzania, and Zimbabwe.

As founder and CEO, Ms. Seele has conceived and implemented several innovative programs that are being used nationally and internationally. This includes The Black Church Week of Prayer for the Healing of AIDS, the premiere program of The Balm in Gilead. Since its inception in 1989, the Black Church Week of Prayer for the Healing of AIDS has engaged more than 15,000 churches throughout the United States.

Ms. Seele is the recipient of numerous congressional citations, honors, and awards. She has received three notable honors from *Essence Magazine*: in the 35th anniversary issue, Ms. Seele was named one of the 35 most beautiful and remarkable women in the world. Susan Taylor, *Essence* editorial director, says these women exemplify the ways *Essence* has defined what it means to be a beautiful black woman: Sprited and Spiritual. In February 2004 Ms. Seele was featured as "One of the New Activists" in the tradition of great African-American heroes, and in October 2003 *Essence* named her one of "50 Women Shaping the World." In 2000 she received the Congressional Black Caucus Award and in 2001 the African American AIDS Policy and Training Institute selected her as a "Hero in the Struggle." She has appeared as an AIDS expert on numerous national and international television and radio networks and has been profiled and quoted in numerous publications, both in the U.S. and abroad.

In May 2006 *Time* magazine honored Pernessa Seele as one of the 100 "people who shape our world" for her work on behalf of AIDS patients.

She is the granddaughter of former Mayor Charles Augustus Seele and the grandniece of former Mayor William Seele, Sr.

Stephen Towns

As a young man growing up in Lincolnville, Stephen Towns had a creative spirit. This spirit was partly inspired by his mother, Patricia, a sweetgrass basket weaver. Stephen attended Ladson Elementary School, Alice Birney Middle School, and R. B. Stall High School, all in the Charleston County School System. While in school, the visual arts became his best means of communication and helped determine his career ambitions. As an adult he has become an accomplished painter and portrait artist. Spritual values infuse all of his work.

Stephen Towns shown here with some of his work.

Stephen attributes much of the meaning of his work to the community in which he was raised. He remarks: "In small communities like the one in which I was raised, people tend to know of, or be familiar with, one another. Everyone has a story and is important in their own right. Unfortunately, our human nature does not allow us to remain constantly aware of that, causing us to devalue others and ourselves. I ask to figuratively tell those stories in my work. In a sense, my work is self-discovery into finding my own identity."

He received a Bachelor of Fine Arts degree from the University of South Carolina in Columbia in May 2004. There, he received the Ed Yaghjian Undergraduate Studio Award in 2003. Stephen has displayed his work in group exhibitions in Columbia and Charleston, notably at the Richland County Public Library and in the Piccolo Spoleto and Moja Arts Festival Juried Exhibitions. In 2003, he was awarded first prize in the Moja Arts Festival and his work is included in the Charleston County collection. In 2005 Towns had his first solo exhibition at the City Gallery at the Dock Street Theatre in Charleston.

Towns currently resides in the Charleston area. Many in the Charleston arts community consider him an exciting up-and-coming artist who will make major contributions in the near future.

Military

The citizens of Lincolnville have always felt a great love for their country. Many of them have demonstrated this through service in the different branches of the Armed Forces. Some served as officers, many served more than twenty years to reach retirement, while others served for shorter terms. The town of Lincolnville is proud of them all.

Among our citizens who have served as officers are Michael German, Rochelle A. Greene, Cherise Jennings, Theodore Sellers, Jr., John Squire, and Clayton Williams.

Colonel John Squire spent his youth in Lincolnville in the late 1940s. He lived with his beloved grandmother, Mrs. Squire. He received his early education at Lincolnville Elementary School and Bonds-Wilson High School in North Charleston. He graduated from South Carolina State College in Orangeburg in 1958 and was commissioned into the U. S. Army. Colonel Squire had a distinguished military career and served in many countries around the world. Since retiring from the U.S. Army, Colonel Squire now lives in Maryland.

Captain Clayton Williams was born in Lincolnville on November 26, 1943. He is the son of the late Christopher E. Williams and Rev. Anna R. Williams. Clayton attended Lincolnville Elementary School, Bonds-Wilson High School, and South Carolina State College. Captain Williams was commissioned into the Army as a lieutenant in 1967 and served his country with honor. He was stationed at Fort Polk, Louisiana, and served in Vietnam.

Captain Williams

Captain Williams served his country on active duty for three years and on reserve duty for seven years. He received the Army Commendation Medal for Leadership, the Expert Infantry Award, and the Award for Vietnam Service.

When Captain Williams left the Army he enrolled in the Medical University of South Carolina in Charleston. After completing his studies he became a chemist and has worked in that field for more than 30 years.

Captain Rochelle A. Greene is the daughter of Stella M. Aiken and the late Samuel Edward Aiken. She received her early education at Lincolnville Elementary School and Bonds-Wilson High School. She graduated from Benedict College in Columbia, South Carolina. She served in the United States Air Force from December 1979 until December 1991.

During this tenure, Captain Greene was assigned as the services operations officer at Charleston Air Force Base (AFB), and Clark Air Base in the Republic of the Philippines, McGuire AFB (N.J.), and Homestead AFB (Fla.). Captain Greene acted as the deputy to the chief/commander of the Service Squadron and ensured quality support services were provided to active duty assigned, transient, retired, and veteran members. The services she oversaw included hotel, dining, laundry, dormitory housing and upgrades, and mortuary affairs for active and retired veterans. Captain Greene served as consumer advocate for the commissary and base exchange operations.

As billeting officer at Clark Air Base, Captain Greene's leadership helped her operation win the Outstanding Innkeeper Award for the Pacific Air Forces Command. As food services officer,

Captain Greene achieved the Food Services Hennessey Award. Both awards were the first every achieved by Clark Air Base. Later, while serving as chief of the services division in Korea, Captain Greene used her unique management style and skills to lead her division to its first Pacific Air Forces Innkeeper and Hennessey Awards in the category of small bases. Consequently it was selected as the Outstanding Unit of the Year for the Pacific Air Forces Command.

Captain Greene

Captain Greene earned service recognition and awards including the Air Force Commendation medal with one bronze oak leaf cluster, the Air Force Outstanding Unit Award, the National Defense Service medal, two Air Force Overseas ribbons (short and long), the Air Force Longevity Service Award ribbon with two bronze oak leaf clusters, the Small Arms Marksmanship expert ribbon, and the Air Force training ribbons. Captain Greene served in support of Operation Desert Shield/Storm from August 2, 1990, to February 23, 1991.

Captain Greene separated from the military in December 1991 to gain more quality time with her family. She is now a social worker and her family resides in Hampton, Virginia.

Captain Cherise Jennings is the daughter of Ernest and Willa Mae Jennings of Lincolnville. Her father served many years on the Lincolnville Town Council. Captain Jennings received her education at Ladson Elementary School, Alice Birney Middle School, and R. B. Stall High School. She graduated from South Carolina State University, where she was commissioned into the

United States Army. She has served with honor at several bases in the United States and continues to serve her country.

Major Theodore Sellers, Jr., is the son of Carrie and Theodore Sellers, Sr., of Lincolnville. Major Sellers received his early education at Ladson Elementary School, Alice Birney Middle School, and R. B. Stall High School. He is a graduate of South Carolina State University. Major Sellers was commissioned into the Army as a lieutenant. He continues to serve his country with honor.

Lieutenant Colonel German

Lieutenant Colonel Michael Lewis German is the son of Elnora German and grandson of Marie and Henry Dezelle. He received his early education at Lincolnville Elementary School and Bonds-Wilson High School. He served honorably in the enlisted ranks for ten years before entering the Reserve Officer Training Corps at Troy State University, Alabama. Colonel German has served in a variety of staff and command positions at the detachment, squadron, MAJCOM, Air Staff, and Office of the Secretary of Defense levels. Some of his awards and decorations are: Republic of Vietnam Campaign Medal, Vietnam Service Medal with one bronze star, National Defense Service Medal with two bronze stars, Air Force Achievement Medal, Air Force Commendation medal with one oak leaf cluster, Defense Meritorious Service Medal, and Air Combat Camera Service Company Grade Officer of the Year Award. He continues to serve his country with honor.

Some of our dedicated military men and women who served our country for 20 years or more as enlisted personnel are Nathan Bennett, Kirby Douglas, Luther Douglas, James Charles Hampton, Dwayne Jacobs, George Jacobs, Miller Ross, James Allen Williams, Jessie Williams, and Sandy M. Williams.

Sgt. First Class Jessie Williams is the son of the late Mary Gardner of Lincolnville. He served in the United States Army for more than 20 years at many bases in the United States and around the world. He now resides in San Antonio, Texas, with his family.

Sgt. First Class Williams

First Sgt. Sandy M. Williams is the son of the late Christopher E. Williams and Rev. Anna R. Williams. He received his education from Lincolnville Elementary School, Bonds-Wilson High School, and Trident Technical College. At the age of 20, he was drafted into the U.S. Army. He served at Fort Jackson (S.C.), Fort Leonardwood (Mo.), Fort Riley (Kan.), Fort Benning (Ga.), and Fort Stewart (Ga.), and in Germany.

In July 1990 Sergeant Williams was assigned to the Republic of Saudi Arabia during Operation Desert Storm/Desert Shield; he spent seven months in a combat zone.

Twenty-two years after entering the army, Sergeant Williams was placed on the Company Sergeant Major/E-9 promotion list, but retired in August 1994. Sergeant Williams received the following awards: Army Service

First Sgt. Williams

Ribbon, Good Conduct Medal, National Defense Service Ribbon, four Army Achievement medals, two Army Commendation medal, three Non-commissioned Officers Professional Development Ribbons, Overseas Service Asian Service Medal, and Liberation and Defense of Kuwait Medal. Sergeant Williams resides in Hinesville, Georgia, with his family.

Chief Master Sgt. James Allen Williams is the son of the late Christopher E. Williams and Rev. Anna R. Williams. He received his education at Lincolnville Elementary School, Bonds-Wilson High School, R. B. Stall High School, and Trident Technical College. He received his Bachelor of Science degree from Southern Illinois University and Master of Arts degree from Webster University.

Chief Master Sgt. Williams

Chief Williams enlisted in the Air Force in 1972 and served at Lackland AFB (Tex.), Charleston AFB, Andrews AFB (Md.), Chanute AFB (Ill.), and Keflavik Naval Air Station, Iceland. He served his country for 27 years.

Chief Williams received the following awards: Air Force Meritorious Service Medal with two oak leak clusters, Air Force Commendation Medal with one oak leaf cluster, Air Force Achievement Medal with three oak leaf clusters, 89th Operation Group Senior Non-Commissioned Officer of the Year, 89th Airlift Wing's nominee for the General Lew Allen Jr. Award, 89th Airlift Wing's nominee for the Lance P. Sijan Award, 1st Helicopter Squadron's Quality Award, Maintenance Person of the Quarter, and the 89th Airlift Wing's Sam Fox Service Award. Chief Williams resides in Clinton, Maryland, with his family.

Chief Master Sergeant James Charles Hampton was born in Mayo, Florida. He is the son of the late Charlie and Louise Hampton of Sanford, Florida. He received his early education at Carbo Elementary, Midway Elementary, Hopper Academy, and Crooms Academy High School. He continued his education after enlisting in the Air Force and earned his Bachelor of Science degree from Southern Illinois University at Carbondale, Master of Science degree from Southern Illinois at Edwardsville, and the Education Specialist degree from The Citadel in Charleston.

Chief Master Sgt. Hampton

Chief Hampton served at Lackland AFB (Tex.), Beale AFB (Cal.), McClellan AFB (Cal.), Forbes AFB (Kan.), Dover AFB (Del.), Charleston AFB, and in Vietnam. He was the first African-American 437th Military Airlift Wing Aircraft Standardization Loadmaster at the Charleston AFB. Chief Hampton traveled the world as an aircraft loadmaster. He retired after serving 23 years.

Chief Hampton received the following awards and decorations: Bronze Star Medal, Meritorious Service Medal, Air Medals with four oak leaf clusters, Air Force Commendation Medal with three Devices, Army Commendation Medal, Armed Forces Expeditionary Medal (Korea, Grenada, Dominican Republic) with two devices, Humanitarian Service Medal with five Devices, National Defense Service Medal, Vietnam Service Medal with three Devices, Air Force Presidential Unit Citation, Navy Presidential Outstanding Unit, Air Force Outstanding Unit Award with three Devices, Republic of Vietnam Gallantry Cross with Devices, Republic of Vietnam Campaign Medal. He was named by the Charleston-area Jaycees one of American's Most Outstanding Men for 1979 and as the 437th Military Airlift Wing Senior Noncommissioned Officer of the Year for 1979.

Chief Hampton began his second career as a teacher at Burke High School in Charleston in August 1985. He later served as assistant principal at Garrett High School and R. B. Stall High School. In 1995 he was appointed principal at Stall and served in that position until he retired in August 2003.

Chief Hampton became a resident of Lincolnville when he married the former Christine Williams of Lincolnville. An active member of the community, he served as chief of the volunteer fire department for seven years and as a member of town council for eighteen years. He is an active member of historic Ebenezer A.M.E. Church.

Seaman Third Class George Jacobs served in the United States Navy for 20 years. He achieved the rank of third class. He traveled to many ports around the world, then returned to Lincolnville after his retirement and served on the Lincolnville town council for sixteen years. His wife, the late Albertha Jacobs, was an active member of the Lincolnville Civic League. He resides in Lincolnville with his children and grandchildren.

Seaman Third Class Jacobs

Burial Site of Chief Ross

Chief Miller Ross retired from the United States Navy after serving more than 20 years. He was married to Ruth Mayes Ross, who served as town clerk for many years. His hobby was building model airplanes and model ships in jars. The children in the community called him the "Ice Cream Man" because he would buy ice cream for all the children in the community. Chief Ross is buried in the military cemetery in Beaufort, South Carolina.

Kirby Douglas

Nathan Bennett is the son of the late Samuel and Mary Bennett. He received his education at Lincolnville Elementary School and Bonds-Wilson High School. He entered the military in 1965 and served his country with honor for 20 years.

Kirby Douglas is the son of the late John and Janie Douglas. He received his education at Lincolnville Elementary and Bonds-Wilson High School. He served in the United States Air Force for more than 20 years.

Luther Douglas is the son of the late John and Janie Douglas. He received his education at Lincolnville Elementary School, Alice Birney Middle School, and R. B. Stall High School. He served 20 years in

Luther Douglas

Chief Dwayne Jacobs

the United States Air Force as a fireman. He enjoys riding his motorcycle.

Dwayne Jacobs is the son of George Jacobs and the late Alberta Jacobs. He has served 20 years in the United States Navy. He received his education at Lincolnville Elementary and Ladson Elementary, Alice Birney Middle School, and R. B. Stall High School. He received the rank of chief and served at many ports around the world.

The following is a listing of many other men and women of Lincolnville who served our country with honor:

Sgt. (E-5) Tyrone Aiken, U.S. Army 1972-1975: Fort Jackson (S.C.), Fort Lee (Va.) and Germany. Army Reserves 1975-1988, U.S. East Coast, Germany.

Tsgt. (E-6) Andrew Carpenter, U.S. Air Force: Lackland AFB (Tex.), Charleston AFB. Temporary duty in Italy, Spain, and Greece.

Corporal Samuel Richard Cox, Sr., U.S. Army 1941-1945: Fort Jackson (S.C.), Fort Benning (Ga.), Aberdeen Proving Ground (Md.), Livingston (La.), and Karachi, India.

Corporal Leroy Daniels, U.S. Army 1951-1955: Fort Bragg (N.C.), Fort Riley (Kan.), Korea, and Japan.

Staff Sgt. (E-5) Frank Dunn, U.S. Air Force 1952-1963: California, England, and Korea.

Buck Sgt. Sherman Glover, U.S. Army 1975-1988: Fort Carson (Colo.), Fort Knox (Ky.), Hunter Airfield (Ga.),

Berlin, Frankfort, and Munich, Germany.

Sgt. Sheri Aiken Jackson, U.S. Air Force 1997 to present: Lackland AFB (Tex.), Goodfellow AFB (Tex.), Langley AFB (Va.), Elmendorf AFB (Ark.), Vandenberg AFB (Cal.), and Bosnia.

Fred Noble, Sr., U.S. Army: Fort Jackson (S.C.), Fort Gordon (Ga.), Fort Bragg (N.C.), Greenland, Arctic Circle.

Staff Sgt. Arnic J. Washington, U.S. Air Force 1954-1957: Lackland AFB (Tex.), Frances E. Warren AFB (Wyo.), Lockbourne AFB (Ohio), Manhattan Beach AFB (N.Y.), George AFB (Cal.), Labrador, and Air Force Reserve.

Sgt. Raymond I. Washington, U.S. Air Force 1980-1988: Lackland AFB (Tex.), Sheppard AFB (Tex.), and Kessler AFB (Miss.). Air National Guard, and Air Force Reserve, England and Japan.

Staff Sgt. (E-5) Clarence Williams, U.S. Air Force 1950s: Lackland AFB (Tex.), Ellington AFB (Tex.), and Alaska.

Many other men and women of Lincolnville have served our country bravely, including:

Clay Aiken, Sr. (Army)
John Baylock (Air Force)
Charles H. Brown (Army)
Albert Burt (Navy)
Samuel Cox, Jr. (Army)
Edward Daniels (Air Force)
Herbert Daniels (Army)
John Douglas (Navy)
Charles Duberry (Marine)
Franklin Duberry (Army)
David Harrison (Army)
Isaac Harrison (Merchant Marine)
Joseph Harrison (Army)
George Jacobs, Jr. (Army)
Ernest Jennings (Army)

Ernest Jennings, Jr. (Army)
Johnny Johnson (Army)
Ralph Linen, Sr. (Marine Corps)
Ralph Linen, Jr. (Marine Corps)
Pamela Mitchell (Army Reserve)
Helene S. Polk (Women's Army Corps)
Ernest Salley (Army)
Michael Salley (Army)
Arthur Singleton (Army)
Booker T. Singleton (Army)
Sofia Smalls (Army)
Gloria Williams (Air Force)
Willie Williams (Army)

Glimpses of the Past

1867 The founders of Lincolnville—Daniel Adger, Marc Buffet, Richard Harvey Cain, Hector Grant, Lewis Ruffin Nichols, Rev. M.B. Salters, and Walter Steele—signed a contract with the South Carolina Railway Company to purchase 620 acres of land for $1,000.00. Though the area was usually called Pump Pond, it was also known as Goose Creek Parish, Lincoln Village, Pon Pon (by natives), the Village of Lincoln, and, finally, Lincolnville.

William Eden started the first Sunday School in his home.

1868 Land was purchased to establish the first church in the village. Richard Cain, Marc Buffet, and William Eden signed the deed for the purchase. During this time the visionaries began organizing a simple form of government (electing an intendant, or mayor), developing a Sunday School, and starting a school.

1878 Ebenezer Church was built.

1880 Ebenezer Church was joined or connected to the African Methodist Episcopal denomination.

1882 The name Lincoln Village was shortened to Lincolnville.

1883 Application was made for a permit to operate a post office. This request was granted and Catherine Wallace, a black woman, was named postmistress.

1885 Charlotte Riley, another black woman, became postmistress on August 20. She is now buried in the Bible Sojourner Cemetery on Greenwood Street in Lincolnville.

Jack Young sold property to Adonis Dezelle on September 25.

1886 The largest earthquake to hit the east coast had three epicenters, two of them near Lincolnville. Damage was most severe for brick, not wooden, buildings, so damage was greater in Charleston than in Lincolnville.

Jack Young sold property to A. Jenkins.

1889 Town officials voted for the town to be incorporated and were granted a charter. Lincolnville was a part of Berkeley County when the charter was granted.

Susan Owens, one of the early settlers, sold property to A. Tony Williams. Other early settlers owning large parcels of property were Marc Buffet, Thomas S. Dennison, Charles A. Seele, David R. Hill, Susan Hammond, Josephine M. Price, Ann Dunmeyer, and William Seele.

Statutes (How To Set up a Town) were approved on December 24.

1891 Marie Eden sold additional property to the Bible Sojourn Society (cemetery). Marie Eden also sold several other parcels of property to many other early settlers. Some of the buyers were:

Elis J. Bellamy	Dianna Frazier	James Keller
Samuel W. Bellamy	Leola Hamilton	Susan Mack
Susan Campbell	John Hill	Cruel Major
Rebecca Dennison	Eliza K. Holman	Judge Milligan
Harriett Fraser	& her children	George O'Neil

John P. Perry
Richard A. Ready
William Peterson
Charles A. Seele
Susan A. Seele & children

Daniel Smith
Martha Steadman
J. S. Steele
Eliza White

1892   R.H. Cain sold property to Samuel Bellamy.

Marie S. Williamson sold property to Jessie Grant.

1893   Henrietta Dickerson sold property to David R. Hill.

Marie S. Williamson sold property to David R. Hill.

1895   Marie S. Williamson sold property to Thomas Pinckney and W. F. Hammond.

1896   Ann Dunmeyer sold property to David R. Hill.

1897   Lucy Burton sold property to Lucy Burton. Date recorded was August 14, 1906.

1898   James Gibbs sold property to Richard A. Ready and to the Lincolnville Emancipation Association.

Marie S. Williamson sold property to Henry Mickens.

Jack Young sold property to Nellie Hardee on June 28, in what was then known as North Lincolnville (now known as Dunmeyer Hill).

1899   Williams Graded School was erected on Pinckney St.

A. Tony Williams served as intendant (mayor).

1901   John Fennick purchased property from the Charleston Investment Company, the Lincolnville Emancipation Association, and Marie S. Williamson.

1902   W. F. Hammond was intendant.

Marie S. Williamson sold property to the Pine Grove (Association) Cemetery and Thomas Dennison.

1903   Amelia Brown sold property to Susan Hammond.

1904   The Lincolnville Emancipation Association sold property to W. F. Hammond on July 10, 1904.

Marie S. Williamson (believed to be Marie S. Eden) sold 51 pieces of property, including one piece to George Keller.

1906   Emmaline Wade sold property to Lucy Burton. Date of record was August 14, 1906. Lucy "Ma" Burton was a remarkable woman who lived in Lincolnville. She was 118 years old when she died in the 1930s. She had been a free person all of her life and had tags to prove this. During the latter part of her life she read the newspaper every day as she smoked her clay pipe. Lucy "Ma" Burton and Charlotte Riley are buried in the Bible Sojourner Cemetery on Greenwood Street in Lincolnville.

1907   Al Causey sold property to W. F. Hammond and also to Susan Hammond.

Marie S. Williamson sold property to Richard Nesbitt.

1908   Jack Young sold property to Eliza Middleton on March 2.

1909   Postmaster for the town was Samuel Holloway.

Marie S. Williamson sold property to J.W. Albright, W. F. Hammond, and Mattie Hill.

1910   Mayor William Seele was serving as intendant.

1911	Marie S. Williamson sold property to Mattie Hill.
1912	Eliza K. Harris sold property to Ebenezer trustees.
	W. F. Hammond served as intendant.
	Charlotte Riley sold property to Ida Robinson.
	Sheriff R. G. Causey sold property to J.W. Albright.
1913	Robert M. Holman sold property to Mattie Hill.
1914	W. F. Hammond served as intendant.
1916	On March 31 the town of Lincolnville passed a resolution to surrender the town charter and accept incorporation.
	A special election was held on May 3, on the question of surrendering the charter and accepting incorporation under the general laws of South Carolina. The eight qualified electors voted yes.
	R. M. McCown, S.C. secretary of state, certified that the town of Lincolnville was duly incorporated with the privileges, powers, and immunities, and subject to the limitations, prescribed in Article I, Chapter XLVIII, Code of 1912.
1919	Jesse Smith sold property to the trustees of Methodist Episcopal Church of Lincolnville.
1920	Charles Augustus Seele was the intendant of Lincolnville. The marshal was Mr. Wilson. Wardens were: W. F. Hammond, Hector Grant, Richard Ready, and Daniel Ben Barron.
1923	Lincolnville (formerly a part of Berkeley County, known as

Goose Creek Parish) became a part of Charleston County.

1924 Lincolnville Elementary School was built on Broad Street on four acres of land.

1933 The town's jail was ordered "shut down" because it had no plumbing or electricity and was found to be unsanitary.

1938 Lincolnville was at risk of losing its charter until town officials informed members of the state legislature that the town planned to bring in electrical power for the citizens.

1940 Joseph Manley served as marshal for the town.

Samuel Keller had a shoe repair business conducted from his home on Meeting Street.

George Chinners owned a grocery store and sold gas. The hand-cranked gas pump was shaped like a lighthouse.

1944 The Cosmopolitan Civic League was organized by a group of women. Louise Hill served as the first president.

1945 Mary Bowman owned a grocery store on Smith Street.

Louise Hill owned a beauty shop, located behind her home on Meeting Street across Dunmeyer Hill Road.

Milkman Martin delivered milk door to door to those who wanted to buy it.

1946 Combined church school and Vacation Bible School picnics were held between Ebenezer and Wesley churches.

Miller's Grocery Store, owned by Leon Miller and

located on Lincolnville Road, sold groceries and gas.

1950 Marshal George Gardner received a salary of $4.00 a week.

1953 Ida Brown Ross owned a beauty shop on Lincolnville Road.

Town Marshal George Gardner died on July 21. George White appointed marshal for the town.

Faculty and students moved to the old Williams Graded School on Pinckney Street (now used as the Town Hall) while the Lincolnville Elementary School was being renovated. Ebenezer A.M.E Church was also used for the upper grades.

Questions were raised concerning relinquishing the town's charter back in 1916.

1954 Sam Bennett appointed marshal.

1955 The train depot was torn down and the passenger train no longer stopped in Lincolnville.

1957 A shoe shop operated on the corner of Pinckney and Railroad Avenue, owned by Samuel Richardson and his daughter Betty.

1959 Portions of Lincolnville Road were paved from Broad Street to the area near the Chick-a-saw Lumber Mill on Owens Drive.

Many young people left town because there were no jobs and not much social life.

1960 Hazel Spells owned a beauty shop and floral shop on the corner of Railroad Avenue and Colpat Street.

1964 George Clayton Mance served as mayor. Wardens: Clay Aiken, Curtis Glover, Samuel Cox, and Richard Drayton. Ruth Ross worked as clerk, and Curtis Glover as finance chairperson.

A passenger train passed through Lincolnville carrying Lady Bird Johnson, wife of President Lyndon Baines Johnson. Town residents gathered as the train went by.

1966 Clay Aiken, a warden, was elected to complete the term of Mayor George Clayton Mance who died before the end of his term. Citizens serving with Mayor Aiken were: Richard Drayton, Curtis Glover, George Jacobs, and Fred Noble, Sr. Mayor Aiken did not run for a second term.

1967 Sam Bennett was the walking marshal. He was paid $16.60 monthly. Charles Bell, the police chief, was paid $100.00 monthly. Luella D. Seele served as clerk.

Charles Ross elected mayor for the first time. Wardens were Willie Brown, Herbert Cook, George Jacobs, and Arnic J. Washington. Luella D. Seele served as clerk.

1969 The title for town council members was changed from wardens to councilmen.

Town Marshal Sam Bennett resigned.

Mayor Ross asked County Council for help completing the fire station and subsidizing police officers' salary.

The town's population was 880, 60% black. The first white town councilman, Rev. F. A. Roberts, was elected.

During this time there was no city water, public sewage system, garbage pick-up, business district, traffic signals, or arms for the railroad crossing. The town had three paved streets and a single general store owned and operated by Leon Miller, Sr.

Tax collection process was put in place.

During the early part of 1969 town meetings were still held in the old Williams Graded School (sometimes called the Old Town Hall). The building was heated by an old woodstove.

Ten mercury-vapor street lights were installed.

An Office of Equal Opportunity was opened in the town. Ida B. Ross and Dorothy B. Glover worked this office, making referrals for legal and economic assistance.

Broyhill Industry, long believed to be out of the town's limits, is actually located in town, according to Mayor Ross. The general manager of Broyhill was unsure about this, though he was quoted: "We will support the town."

Charles Bell, the town's only full-time policeman, resigned twice because he had not been paid.

During this time, Mayor Ross made his first of many contacts with U.S. Senator Strom Thurmond.

Lincolnville Elementary School—built in 1924, and remodeled in 1956—was closed due to integration of county schools. Faculty and staff at that time were: Eugene Willis, principal; teachers Geraldine Fields, Mildred S. Cox, Luella D. Seele, and Rosalee W. Washington. Lucille R. Noble was librarian.

1970 Nathaniel P. Hardee was hired as policeman. Rosalee W. Washington served as acting clerk until August 1970 when Vermel B. Glover was hired as town clerk.

Gamerlear Williams served as chief of the volunteer fire department.

After two years of service on council, F. A. Roberts decided to run for mayor. He was defeated by 13 votes.

Council members serving during Mayor Ross's second term in office were: Samuel Cox, Sr., Harold Douglas, George Jacobs, and Arnic Washington. Willie Brown, who served during the first term, died.

Some of the accomplishments made during Mayor Ross's second term: construction of the recreation complex, Fire Department organized, Lincolnville Elementary School purchased and converted into a municipal complex, wrought iron railing (designed by Philip Simmons) installed on the portico of the Municipal Complex, street signs purchased by the Civic League were installed, and almost 200 acres of land were annexed to the town.

Mail service switched from Lincolnville Circle to curbside delivery.

New town codes put in place.

Election laws changed so that new mayor and council would be elected from a full slate for four years.

Police officer Charles Bell resigned because of the low salary. Rosalee W. Washington again acted as clerk when Vermel Glover resigned.

1971 A resolution to change the laws regarding the elections for mayor and council was accepted by the S.C. General Assembly, after being filed with the S.C. Election

Commission. The law established that elections would be held every four years rather than every two.

A Lincolnville town councilman who served as police commissioner was shot by the Lincolnville police chief during an argument at the chief's home. The commissioner and another councilman had gone to the chief's home to demand the return of all town equipment, in effect firing the chief. The chief was charged with assault and battery with intent to kill and was arrested.

1972 Levi Duberry hired as town clerk and treasurer.

Mayor Charles Ross was appointed to a one-year term on the South Carolina and Local Government Advisory Committee for Region IV. This committee made recommendations on how best to attract and utilize state and local government resources such as money, manpower, materials, and information.

The Lincolnville police chief charged with assault and battery with intent to kill was convicted and incarcerated. Bernard Fielding, Esq., represented the town.

1973 Myra A. Washington participated in the Miss Black Teenage South Carolina Beauty Pageant, representing Lincolnville, at the Gaillard Municipal Auditorium in Charleston. She was sponsored by Christine W. Hampton and Edna Elaine Glover.

1974 Lincolnville government changed when S.C. Rep. Robert Woods's bill in the General Assembly allowed small towns to change from mayor and four councilmen to mayor and six councilmen.

Kay Tager was elected to serve as chairperson of finance committee.

Mayor Ross won reelection, though he was challenged by candidate Betty Seabrook Hardee, whose slate included council candidates Leola Holmes, F. A. Roberts, and Josh Bell. The challenge was dismissed. Mayor Ross and council members were installed: Samuel Cox, Harold Douglas, George Jacobs, Kay Tager, Arnic J. Washington, and Joe Weaver. Zelma Fielding was hired as clerk-treasurer when Levi Duberry, Jr., resigned.

1975 Town Council installed shelves in a room in the Municipal Building to be used as a library.

1976 The mayor-council form of government, with six council members, was retained. Under this system, the mayor works in the dual capacity as a legislative member of council and in an executive capacity as chief administrator of the council's policies.

1977 Leo Pavlovich hired as policeman.

William Montgomery served as superintendent of the streets.

1978 Norman Craven replaced Kay Tager on Town Council. Arnic J. Washington elected mayor pro-tem.

Election laws amended so that council members' terms were staggered every two years. This ensured experienced leadership on council.

Responding to a reporter's question as to citizens in the town being prejudiced towards each other, Mayor Ross stated: "Let's face it, you are white and I'm black and we've both got a certain amount of prejudices about each other. You show me somebody who doesn't—he dead as hell."

1979　Lincolnville Elementary School property deeded to the town of Lincolnville for $1.00. The facility was then used as the Town Hall and community center.

The fire station was completed in May.

Council members: Samuel Cox, Norman Craven, Leroy Daniels, George Jacobs, Arnic J. Washington, and Joe Weaver.

1980　Notification that Lincolnville's Williams Graded School was added to the National Register of Historic Places was received from the Department of the Interior by the South Carolina Department of Archives and History. The nomination was prepared by the Historic Preservation Survey and Registration Division of the SCDAH and Elias Bull of the Berkeley-Charleston-Dorchester Council of Governments. The building was one of the few known examples of S.C. public buildings associated with 19th- and early 20th-century black history. Although the building was owned by the Town of Lincolnville, it was used for worship services by the Friendship Church of God and Christ.

Swearing-in ceremony of newly elected officials: Mayor Charles Ross, Council members Charles Duberry, Leland Shannon, and Arnic J. Washington. Other officials retaining their seats were Norman Craven, Leroy Daniels, and Joe Weaver.

Arnic J. Washington elected mayor pro-tem. Anthony O'Neil, Esq., named town attorney, James Hampton fire chief, and Zelma Fielding clerk-treasurer.

1981　Kirk Meyers, Esq., hired to represent the town as attorney.

Groundbreaking ceremony held for the Lincolnville water system.

1982 Mayor Ross met with U.S. Senator Strom Thurmond to solicit help in getting financial aid for the town's law-enforcement department.

J. B Wagoner elected assistant fire chief.

1983 Mayor Charles Ross was invited to dine with President Ronald Reagan.

Donnie White hired as police officer.

Mayor Ross resigned after 17 years of service to the town. However, with seven months left to fulfill his term, the mayor was still working on projects he wanted to accomplish. He changed his mind and decided to remain in office after many residents asked him to rescind his resignation.

The mayor's first priority for the town is the completion of the water system.

At age 65, Mayor Ross was still working hard at preserving the town's heritage. Before World WarII, Lincolnville's population was about 98% black. Now the town of almost 900 is almost racially balanced.

Councilman Leroy Daniels elected mayor pro tem.

Town of Lincolnville awarded $25,000 of the $250,000 requested from Community Block Grants.

Town will not receive cable television service as anticipated. The only bid received required pre-engineering work which the town could not afford.

1984 Local officials and some other government officials got a glimpse of what could be future plans pertaining to a waste treatment system.

Council members: Tyrone Aiken, Charles Duberry, Annette D. Goodwin, Mary Williams, Alfred Baylock, and Leroy Daniels.

Michele Gleaton crowned "The First Miss Lincolnville."

1985 Town Officials: Charles Ross, mayor; Council members Tyrone Aiken, Charles Duberry, Annette Douglas Goodwin, Mary Williams, Alfred Baylock, and Leroy Daniels; Sandra F. Lary, clerk.

1986 No tax increase.

Councilman James Hampton elected mayor pro-tem. Councilman Tyrone Aiken withdrew from the nomination for the office because of an annexation conflict regarding the area where he lived.

1988 Zelma Fielding elected mayor in an unopposed candidacy, the first woman ever to hold the office. She replaced Charles Ross who stepped down for health reasons after serving for 21 years.

1989 Former Mayor Charles Ross died on Thursday, July 20. He was eulogized on July 24, at Ebenezer A.M.E. Church. Town officials: Zelma Fielding, mayor; Council members Tyrone Aiken, Charles Bell, Charles Duberry, Tommy Skinner, James Hampton, and Alfred Baylock; Sandra Lary, clerk; Donnie White, police officer.

Hurricane Hugo left citizens without water, electricity, and partial telephone services for approximately two weeks. The town's residents were very appreciative of help provided by people around the country.

A small group of town residents gathered with Mayor Fielding to celebrate the town's 100th birthday. Some notable guests were Hillary Douglas, member of the Charleston County School Board, who grew up in Lincolnville, and Mrs. Ida Brown Ross, widow of the former mayor. Hillary Douglas spoke briefly on the history of his hometown and the changes it had made over the years. The United States Navy Band played the national anthem and a prelude before the ceremony. Several long-time residents reminisced about their childhood years in the community. Another highpoint of the celebration was Mayor Fielding's "Lincolnville Perspective" for the town's next century. She concluded the celebration by stating, "We may not realize our dreams tomorrow, but we are developing affirmative strategies for economic and social development as we move into the next century."

1990 Town officials: Zelma Fielding, mayor; Council members Tyrone Aiken, Charles Bell, Charles Duberry, (mayor pro tem), Ernest Jennings, Annette Douglas (who resigned before her term was completed), Samuel Jacobs, and Alfred Baylock.

Special election held. Charles T. Buggs and Laverne Williams were elected to fill the vacant seats of Annette Douglas Goodwin and Samuel Jacobs. They served through April 1994.

Enoch Dickerson served as judge for the town.
Mayor Fielding threatened to resign. Charles Buggs, mayor pro tem, believed the mayor was frustrated by lack of funds and cooperation.

Mayor Fielding proclaimed December 6 as Arbor Day.

The group "Releaf" donated a tree to be planted at Town Hall.

The town's first Christmas tree lighting celebration was sponsored by the Civic League.

1991 The Civic League sponsored the first Independence Day parade.

1992 Citizens and volunteers brought in by the Charleston County Sheriff's Office worked together to rebuild the recreation area damaged by Hurricane Hugo.

Town officials: Zelma Fielding, mayor; Council members Tyrone Aiken, Charles Bell, Charles Duberry, Charles Buggs, Laverne Williams, and Alfred Baylock.

The Civic League sponsored Pride Week during a Clean-up Campaign. Crime Watch Committee organized block captains and installed Crime Watch signs.

After the election in April, the new elected officials were: Charles Buggs, mayor; Council members Tyrone Aiken, Charles Duberry, Alfonso Green (mayor pro tem), James Hampton, Laverne Williams, and Sam Williams; Linda Grooms, clerk, and Sonia Glover, billing clerk.

Denise RaeShawn Gleaton served as Miss Lincolnville.

Town Council, on Judge Enoch Dickerson's recommendation, voted to name the Town Hall building in honor of former Mayor Charles Ross. Dedication service planned for December 12, 1993. Crime Watch committee purchased monument and plaque in his honor.

Mayor Buggs's request for a Lincolnville Exit sign on Interstate 26 was denied.

1993   Sherri Aiken served as Miss Lincolnville. Zanitha M. Dickerson was her attendant.

Lincolnville's proposed budget for the year 1993-1994 was to increase by nearly 55 percent, though the property tax rate would drop 6 percent for town residents. The first reading of the proposed $164,000 budget was approved. The budget also included salaries for two part-time policemen, a town clerk, and a fund of $12,636.

1994   Council voted to give the Civic League $500 to pay for the first "Welcome to Lincolnville" sign.

Town officials: Charles Buggs, mayor; Council members James Hampton (mayor pro tem), Andrew Carpenter, Alfonso Green, Ernest Jennings, Leland Shannon, and Charles Duberry.

Sonia Glover, billing clerk, resigned on August 24 and was replaced by Ernestine Devine.

Jean Weidman appointed election commissioner. Rosalee W. Washington and John Connors served on this committee.

The mayor's salary was $4,800 annually, but was recommended in proposed budget to increase to $13,500 annually. Council members' salaries would increase to $1,200 annually.

Lincolnville's mayor, council members, and some residents met with Summerville officials about concerns for 12 acres of land to be sold to Suburban Disposal Waste Service. Carla Locklear and Mayor Buggs led the Lincolnville residents in opposing the change in rezoning because the company is a noise nuisance, rodents would breed in the trash, and the habitat of the wildlife would be disturbed. Mayor Buggs stated that since Suburban only wanted the land as a buffer, he was requesting reconsideration of rezoning the property. The property was zoned to be used only as a buffer.

1995 Mayor Buggs stated at the October council meeting that the millage for that year would be 110 mills, down from 112 mills last year.

Directional signs for the town of Lincolnville were erected on Interstate 26 by the South Carolina Highway Department. The signs directed motorists through downtown Summerville, onto Richardson Avenue, and then to Lincolnville.

Christmas tree lighting celebration sponsored by the Civic League on December 17.

1996 Town officials and their duties: Charles Buggs, mayor; Council members James Hampton (zoning), Ernest Jennings (Police Department), Charles Duberry (Fire Department), Leland Shannon (Public Buildings and Streets), Alfonso Green (Water), and Dorothy Bailey (Health Department).

Mayor Charles Buggs received an invitation to attend President William Jefferson Clinton's birthday celebration, but he could not attend.

Mayor Buggs organized a Mayor's Advisory Council. Members of the council were J. B. Wagoner, Rosalee W. Washington, and Mary Williams.

Comprehensive Planning Committee established. Residents serving on this committee were Roosevelt Brown, Barbara Dease, Christine W. Hampton, Martina Jacobs, Laverne Williams, and Rosalee W. Washington.

Facilitators were Becky Ford, Kathryn Basha, and Emmet Barlowe from the Council of Government.

Judge Enoch Dickerson administered the oath of office to install Mayor Buggs and council members James Hampton, Alfonso Green, and Leland Shannon who were reelected to serve.

1997 The Civic League sponsored Pride Week as a clean-up campaign. All citizens were invited to clean their yards and streets. Street captains were listed in the newsletter/water bill.

Ballfield and scoreboard named in honor of Leonard Turner, a resident who started Lincolnville's first baseball league.

May Day festival sponsored by Crime Watch committee. Flashing lights and railroad crossing arms were installed at Dunmeyer Hill Road and Pinckney Street railroad crossing.

1998 On January 21 a groundbreaking ceremony was held for the Lincolnville Elderly Garden Apartments on Slidel Street.

Leroy Daniels, a former councilman, suggested that the town keep the "old jail" as an historic site. A Comprehensive Land Use Plan committee agreed.

The Civic League sponsored Law Enforcement Day. On display were the City of Charleston police helicopter, police horses, and the Camaro police car. This activity was sponsored in conjunction with the summer lunch program.

1999 "Welcome to Lincolnville" sign, donated by the Civic

League, was installed. Bricks were donated by Boral Brick Company at the request of council member Dorothy Bailey.

Adopt a Highway clean-up project started.

Civic League worked with State Heritage Corridor planners to be placed on the state Heritage Trail.

Current town officials and staff: Charles Buggs, mayor; Council members Tyrone Aiken, Charles Duberry, Alfonso Green, James Hampton, Ernest Jennings, and Leland Shannon; Linda Grooms, clerk; Fire Chief Charles Gantt and Police Officer Kenneth Vann.

The town's Fire Department received a Mack truck from North Charleston.

Brochures with a short history of the town were delivered to all citizens inviting them to the annual Christmas tree lighting celebration sponsored by the Civic League.

Town of Lincolnville Comprehensive Land Use Plan completed. Current members of Planning Commission: Dorothy Bailey, Roosevelt Brown, Barbara Dease, Christine W. Hampton, Mary Howell, Martina Jacobs, Rosalee W. Washington, Jean Weidman, and Laverne Williams. The work was prepared with the assistance of the Berkeley-Charleston-Dorchester Council of Governments. The Comprehensive Plan was adopted April 27 by the Lincolnville Town Council.

Current town officials: Tyrone Aiken, mayor; Council members Dorothy Bailey, Charles Duberry, James Hampton, Ernest Jennings, Leland Shannon, and Anna Ruth Williams Gleaton.

Crime Watch Committee recognized high school and college graduates and presented them with a monetary gift.

Crime Watch sponsored a Back to School Party in August for the children and in November they distributed Thanksgiving baskets to the needy.

Council member Anna Ruth Williams Gleaton, chairperson of the Health Department, sponsored a Mobile Medical Unit Health Fair.

The Civic League sponsored the Tri-County Summer Lunch Program along with educational activities.

The town received a block grant from the Community Development Block Grant for the first phase of the Lincolnville Public Safety Building.

2001 Mail collection box installed on Town Hall grounds.

Mayor Tyrone Aiken gave the State of the Town address.

Plans were in progress for the new Public Safety Building. Phase One: Purchase of property and design of building. Phase Two: Construction.

Planning and Zoning Committee began the work of updating zoning laws. Committee members: Marshall Kelly (chairperson), Rosalee W. Washington (assistant chairperson), Levern Locklear (secretary), Fred Noble, Sr., Laverne Williams, Donovan Jordan, and Ruth Roberts. When Locklear resigned as secretary, he was succeeded by Ruth Roberts.

A Civic League member inquired about the plans to improve the Bible Sojourn Cemetery in Lincolnville.

The mayor stated that nothing was being done. The area is still damaged after the devastation of Hurricane Hugo. An agreement was made for CARTA to provide bus transportation from Lincolnville to the North Charleston and Charleston areas.

A Zoning Board of Appeals was organized. Members were Laverne Nichols, Robert Cheverie, Sarah Deweese, Allen McDonald, and Gerri Pressley.

Trial of C&B Fire Department vs. Lincolnville Volunteer Fire Department concerned areas to be covered. Trial was heard by Judge Falcon Hawkins.

During a "Boot Drive," Lincolnville firemen collected $3,200 for New York firefighters injured in the September 11 terrorist attack.

A letter was drafted and sent to Ebenezer A.M.E. Church from the Town of Lincolnville requesting a land swap. The land then owned by the church would be used to build the proposed Public Safety Facility.

2002 Mayor Aiken considered accepting the offer from North Charleston Water and Sewer District to handle the billing and collection of fees to Lincolnville's customers. The proceeds would be submitted to the town. Councilman Hampton suggested letting the Public Works Advisory Committee look at the advantages and disadvantages of allowing the North Charleston Sewer District to handle this job.

A Steering Committee for the Town Festival was appointed, with $1,000 allocated for the planning phase. Sonia Glover was appointed chairperson. This was the beginning of the Heritage Festival.

Final ruling from Judge Hawkins regarding C&B Fire Department vs. Lincolnville Volunteer Fire Department: C&B will be responsible for areas previously covered by the Lincolnville Fire Department. This will have a positive effect on insurance rates for homeowners in the town.

Judge Enoch Dickerson resigned as the town's municipal judge. He was replaced by Virgil Deas.

At a special town meeting, Councilman Leland Shannon made a motion to approve the purchase of one acre of property from Ebenezer A.M.E. Church. All present, Dorothy Bailey, Barbara Dease, Charles Duberry, James Hampton, and Leland Shannon, voted in the affirmative.

Cathy Rhodes served as code enforcer. Charles Duberry elected mayor pro tem.

Police Officer Richard Hill resigned.

Mayor Aiken reported to council that the Leland cypress in front of the Town Hall (presented by the Civic League) was removed because it was diseased. The tree will be replaced but placed in a new location.

Ebenezer A.M.E. Church trustees presented a request to council for rezoning of East Pinckney and East Green streets. The request was approved by the Planning and Zoning Committee on October 2. By rezoning from rural residential to conventional neighborhood, the property could be subdivided into two parcels and Ebenezer would be able to purchase the lot adjacent to the church.

2003 Council member Anna Ruth Williams Gleaton was reappointed representative to Charleston County Elected

Official Association.

Barbara Bell appointed municipal town clerk in February.

The Richard Harvey Cain Award established. Sonia Glover was the first recipient.

Frank Dunn's poem "Oh Lincolnville" adopted as the official poem for the town.

A grant from the Berkeley-Charleston-Dorchester Council of Governments was received to construct sidewalks. This was expected to improve the appearance of the Gateway to the town. The paving will be done in three phases.

Web site designed for the town.

Town of Lincolnville Housing Council created.

Interior of the auditorium of the Charles Ross Municipal Complex was remodeled and decorated with blue and gold drapes. The historical African-American pictures were re-hung after being saved from destruction by Councilman James Hampton. The Civic League had the pictures framed by Charles Morris, a teacher at Ladson Elementary School, at no cost to the town.

Ground-breaking celebration for the Lincolnville Senior Community Building was held on December 15. This event was sponsored by the Lowcountry Housing and Economic Development Foundation, Inc.

2004 Mayor Aiken gave his State of the Town address on February 4. He reported on the mid-year budget review, status of all departments, and announced that he would seek a second term.

The zoning ordinance of the Town of Lincolnville was amended to prohibit heavy vehicles and/or heavy trailers on the streets located in the town. This recommendation was presented to Town Council. Trucks were allowed to drive through town, but could not be parked on town streets.

Public Safety Facility ribbon-cutting ceremony held March 19. Groundbreaking ceremony for sidewalk project held the same day at Lincoln Avenue and West Pine Street. Public hearings on May 5 concerned (1) Adoption of Ordinance Amendment to the Light Industrial Zoning District, (2) Petition to Annex 17.5 acres.

Elliot Constantine of Constantine & Constantine Architects, Inc., donated $300 to town recreation program upon completion of the Public Safety Building.

Mayor Aiken announced his appointment to the Charleston Area Transportation Enhancement Committee.

Municipal Judge Virgil Deas administered the oath of office to Mayor Aiken and the three newly elected council members: Dorothy Bailey, James Hampton, and Leland Shannon.

Alec Brebner of the Council of Government made a brief presentation to Town Council and citizens regarding an ordinance to establish a "Planned Development Zoning District."

Lincolnville police assisted in the arrest of a fugitive, charged with the attempted murder of an Oregon deputy sheriff.

Melinda Lucka, Esq., chosen to provide legal counsel to the town and to enter appearances in all active cases and special proceedings, and to conduct suits in which the Town of Lincolnville would be involved.

The application for $57,000 for the conceptual planning of the drainage system was approved.

The property needed for the Boundary Street Extension was discussed with Wither's Industries.

The code enforcement officer's position was vacant.

North Charleston Sewer District discussed the feasibility of extending their sewer lines throughout the town.

Council member Gleaton stated that Phases II and III had been approved for the continuation of sidewalks on Lincoln Avenue, scheduled for October 2004.

Mayor Aiken read a letter of resignation from Sonia Glover, the appointed chairperson of the Cultural and Heritage Festival Committee.

Communication was received from Pamela Queeman, Blessed Vision Ministry's Church administrator, thanking the town for the use of the auditorium in their time of need for a place to worship.

A Look Into the Future

A glimpse into the future of Lincolnville shows a beautiful, clean, thriving town that will grow from the roots laid down a century and a half ago. Records show that the original settlement was divided into four-acre lots with well-kept yards. There were also laws in place and enforced to keep the town orderly and clean. That same concern for the beauty and safety of Lincolnville will extend into the future.

The town will be graced by a lovely "Town Gateway" - aesthetically pleasing to the citizens as well as to those visiting or just passing through our town. It will tell people they are entering a special place.

In the future, the city will emanate from a Town Center, including shopping areas with all of the necessities for the convenience of the citizens such as clothing, food, gas, and family healthcare facilities.

The existing quality of life will be further enhanced and preserved by controlling and managing the commercial and residential growth of the town.

The unique character of the town will be maintained by implementation of employment opportunities, recreational activities, and programs that will encourage all citizens to participate in continuing-education and cultural programs. With an increase in the town's educational level, the poverty level will decrease. Decreasing the poverty level will benefit the entire town.

Some small businesses such as specialty shops in the Town Center and a limited number of large businesses in the designated zoned areas will provide jobs for those wanting to work in their neighborhoods. These businesses will help provide a tax base to support town's economy. However, because of the close proximity of Lincolnville to Summerville, Moncks Corner, North Charleston, and the City of Charleston, citizens also will be able to seek employment in these areas. The town's specialized training programs will help citizens prepare themselves and their families for the higher-paying jobs that will be offered by companies moving into the surrounding areas.

In the future, there will also be paved streets with sidewalks throughout the town. Some of the streets will be widened to accommodate the increased traffic. Traffic signals will be placed at strategic main arteries. Public transportation will be readily available because of the growth of the town and surrounding areas.

The Public Safety Department will double in size and the department's facility will have sleeping areas upstairs. There will be new fire trucks and double the number of volunteers, and the police department will have officers on duty 24 hours a day. They will have new cars loaded with the equipment necessary for all occasions.

All of the churches in town will have life-center facilities and/or new buildings to house their growing memberships and provide educational, spiritual, and recreational programs. In addition to activities provided by the churches, there will also be a public library and museum. The museum will have displays of historical artifacts collected from Lincolnville citizens.

A glimpse into the future of Lincolnville shows a community of people of many races and ages with diverse backgrounds working together to continue what was started many years ago. This will be a community of people working together to develop citizens who are spiritual, social, cultured, and well-rounded. Just as Lincolnville boasts a unique history in which citizens have courageously faced countless challenges for a century and a half, so too will we move forthrightly into our future, developing a town of which our founders and ancestors would be proud.

Lincolnville's past, as this book makes clear, is exceedingly rich. But her future is even richer.

Oh Lincolnville

Frank Dunn

The last bugle has sounded
at the ending of the war,
Where men of North and South had fought
with honor and with valor,
Now brothers were united
and slavery's chains were freed,
A new birth of our country
blest by God's own creed.

Seven men of color had a dream
where men could live and toil,
Among the stately pines that stand
enriched in fertile soil,
Soil that had been nurtured
by those who fought and died,
Oh Lincolnville, Oh Lincolnville
what heritage and pride.

Many years have come and gone
and generations passed,
Have left for us a legacy
that'll never be surpassed,
Black and white, rich and poor
will live in harmony
Ordained by God in Heaven above
that all men should be free.

Lincolnville, Oh Lincolnville
blest by God's own hand,
Long may you live in peace and love
throughout your hallowed land.
Love for all your neighbors
in spite of race and color,
A place where all men can be free
and live in peace once more.

*In 2003 the Lincolnville Town Council adopted a resolution to make
"Oh Lincolnville" the official Town Poem.*

About the Authors

Christine W. Hampton

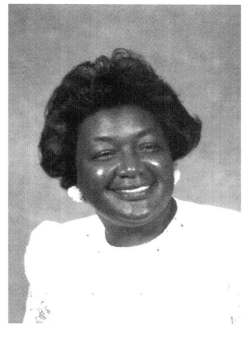

Christine Williams Hampton was born in Lincolnville and has lived there most of her life. She is the fifth of eight children of the late Christopher Elijah Williams and Rev. Anna Rebecca Williams. Christine is married to James Charles Hampton, a member of the Lincolnville Town Council. She is the proud mother of two children, James Christopher and Jade Christine, and stepmother of Tanya Michelle Hampton.

Christine graduated from Lincolnville Elementary School and Bonds-Wilson High School. She continued her education and graduated from South Carolina State College in Orangeburg where she received the Bachelor of Science degree in Elementary Education and her Master of Education degree. She did further studies at The Citadel and the College of Charleston and earned 30 hours of credit beyond the Master's level.

Christine taught third grade for 30 years in the Charleston County School System before retiring in June 1997.

She is a dedicated worker in her church and community. She was a Sunday School teacher at Ebenezer A.M.E. Church for many years. She sings with the Jubilee Choir, which she directs. She works tirelessly on the Trustee Board where she led the project to help restore this 127-year-old historic church.

As a community leader, she has served as president of the Lincolnville Civic League for many years. She works very hard to record the history of Lincolnville with her sister, Rosalee W. Washington. She is also a member in the National Council of Negro Women. She is a charter member of the Sigma Upsilon Omega chapter of Alpha Kappa Alpha sorority and a member of the Lincolnville Quilters.

She helped write the grant to secure the Lincolnville water system and the grant that enabled the Civic League to purchase signs to motivate citizens to work together on beautification projects for the town. She served on the Lincolnville Comprehensive Planning Board to establish a Town Land Use Plan.

Rosalee W. Washington

Rosalee Williams Washington is the daughter of the late Christopher Elijah Williams and Rev. Anna Rebecca Williams. She is married to Arnic J. Washington, who served on the Lincolnville Town Council for many years. They have two children, Myra W. Dyson and Raymond I. Washington, and six grandchildren.

Rosalee graduated from Lincolnville Elementary School and Bonds-Wilson High School. She received her Bachelor of Science degree from South Carolina State College in Orangeburg and a Master degree in School Administration from The Citadel in Charleston.

She taught in the Charleston County School System for 31 years and was named Teacher of the Year at Ladson Elementary School.

A former member of historic Ebenezer A.M.E. Church in Lincolnville, in 1963 she joined Wesley United Methodist Church in Ladson where her husband was already a member. As a member of Wesley Church, she has served in many capacities, including the Wesley Senior Choir, Sunday School, Nurture chairperson, coordinator of Age-level and Family Ministries, president of United Methodist Women, Drama Ministry, and as a Class Leader.

Rosalee is past president of the Lincolnville Civic League, a life member of the National Council of Negro Women, a Chartered Member of the Sigma Upsilon Omega chapter of Alpha Kappa Alpha sorority, and a member of Lily Chapter #134 of the Order of Eastern Stars.

Rosalee is a tireless worker in Lincolnville. She helped write the grant to secure the town water system and a grant to help the Civic League purchase signs to encourage citizens to work together on beautification projects. She was also instrumental in restarting the Summer Lunch Program. She served on the Mayor's Advisory Board during Mayor Charles Bugg's administration. She also served on the Lincolnville Comprehensive Planning Board, the Zoning Board and the Election Commission.

Her hobbies include quilting, reading, writing songs and poetry, and researching the history of Lincolnville.

Photo Credits

SUBJECT (page)	SOURCE
Front cover:	
Lincolnville Elementary School Students and Staff (ca. 1944)	Rev. Anna R. Williams
Back cover:	
Richard Harvey Cain	Lincolnville Town Records
Graduation 1949	Rev. Anna R. Williams
Charles Ross	Lincolnville Town Records (from *Charleston News & Courier*)
Richard Harvey Cain (8)	Lincolnville Town Records
Lewis Ruffin Nichols (11)	Lewis Ruffin Noisette
Lewis Ruffin Nichols family (12)	Lewis Ruffin Noisette
Intendant Williams's Signature (14)	Lincolnville Town Records
Intendant Hammond's Signature (15)	Lincolnville Town Records
Intendant Seele's Signature (16)	Lincolnville Town Records
Charles A. Seele (18)	Helena Polk
Mose Jerome Washington (18)	Ebenezer A.M.E. Church
Intendant Seele and Wardens (19)	Rev. Anna Williams
Clayton Mance (20)	Clayton Mance, Jr.
Clay Aiken	Bernice Aiken
Charles Ross with President Carter (21)	Town of Lincolnville
Charles Ross (23)	Lincolnville Town Records (from *Charleston News & Courier*)
Government Document (25)	Lincolnville Town Records
Zelma Fielding (29)	Lincolnville Town Records
Charles Buggs (31)	Charles Buggs
Tyrone Aiken (33)	James Hampton
Mayor Aiken and Council (34)	James Hampton
Cornerstone (39)	Elias Bull files, Charleston County Public Library
First Lincolnville School (40)	Charleston County School District Archives
Williams Graded School (41)	Elias Bull files, Charleston County Public Library

Photo Credits

Mattie E. Seabrook and Sadie Boags (41)	Louise Hill
Lincolnville Elementary School Students and Staff (42)	Rev. Anna R. Williams
Original Lincolnville Elementary School (44)	Charleston County School Archives
Majorette Uniform (45)	Dorothy Glover
Program Cover (46)	Dorothy Glover
James A. Williams (47)	Rev. Anna R. Williams
Graduation 1960 (48)	Rosalee W. Washington
Graduation 1949 (48)	Rev. Anna R. Williams
Graduation 1950 (49)	Rev. Anna R. Williams
Lincolnville Elementary School Today (49)	James Hampton
Graduation Program (50)	Rev. Anna R. Williams
School Song (51)	Rosalee W. Washington
Ebenezer A.M.E. Church (53)	Rev. Anna W. Gleaton
Ebenezer A.M.E. Church Deed (54)	Tyrone Aiken
Ebenezer A.M.E. Church Senior Choir (55)	Rev. Anna R. Williams
Rev. Josh Gadsden (56)	Dorothy Glover
Rev. Bennett and Members (57)	Rev. Anna R. Williams
Rev. Corbin and Choir (58)	Rev. Anna W. Gleaton
Rev. Jeremiah McKinley (59)	James Hampton
Christening (60)	James Hampton
Ebenezer A.M.E. Church (61)	James Hampton
Sunday School (ca. 1950) (64)	Rev. Anna R. Williams
Nicole, Jade, and Katura (65)	James Hampton
Ryan and Jade (65)	James Hampton
Sunday School (66)	James Hampton
"TEAM" shirts (68)	James Hampton
Sunday School 2000 (69)	James Hampton
Wesley Methodist Episcopal Church (75)	James Hampton
Wesley's Chandelier (71)	Rosalee W. Washington
Wesley's Organ (71)	Rosalee W. Washington
Wesley Church Members (72)	Pernessa Seele
Mt. Zion Baptist Church (73)	James Hampton
Nazareth Holiness Church (76)	James Hampton
Friendship Church of God (78)	James Hampton
Lydia Baptist Church (80)	James Hampton
Joseph Manley (81)	Emily Nelson
Lincolnville's Old Jail (82)	James Hampton
Officer Vann and Mayor Buggs (82)	James Hampton
Judge Dickerson and Miss Crime Watch (83)	James Hampton
Officer Hill and Constables (83)	James Hampton
Officer Vann and Law Enforcement Day (84)	James Hampton

Volunteer Firemen (87)	James Hampton
Fire Stations (88)	James Hampton
Arnic Washington (90)	Christine Hampton
Officials at Christmas Tree Lighting (91)	Christine Hampton
Miss Lincolnville and Miss Flame (92)	James Hampton
David and Louise Hill (93)	Louise Hill
Town Sign (94)	Rosalee W. Washington
Myra Washington (94)	Rosalee W. Washington
Independence Day (94)	Christine Hampton
Miss Lincolnville (Denise) (95)	Rev. Anna W. Gleaton
Miss Lincolnville (Michelle) (95)	James Hampton
Rev. Anna R. Williams (96)	Rev. Anna R. Williams
Yard of Month Sign (96)	James Hampton
Health Fair (98)	James Hampton
Wilhemenia Barron (99)	Rev. Anna R. Williams
James Christopher Hampton (101)	James C. Hampton
David Seabrook Hill and Family (103)	Louise Hill
Rev. Alonzo Holman (104)	Rev. Alonzo Holman
Dr. Lawrence James (107)	Dr. Lawrence James
John Henry McCray (109)	South Caroliniana Library, University of South Carolina
Rachel McCray (110)	Rosalee W. Washington
Richard A. Ready (111)	Naomi Bacote
Charlotte S. Riley (113)	Attorney Ruth Cupp, Dr. Crystal Lucky
Pernessa C. Seele (117)	Steve J. Sherman
Stephen Towns (119)	Stephen Towns
Clayton Williams (122)	Clayton Williams
Rochelle Greene (123)	Stella Aiken
Michael German (124)	Michael German
Jessie Williams (125)	Mary Williams
Sandy Williams (125)	Sandy Williams
James Williams (126)	James Williams
James Hampton (127)	James Hampton
George Jacobs, Sr. (128)	George Jacobs, Sr.
Burial Site of Miller Ross (128)	James Hampton
Kirby Douglas (129)	Geraldine Williams
Luther Douglas (129)	Geraldine Williams
Dwayne Jacobs (130)	James Hampton
Christine W. Hampton (165)	Christine Hampton
Rosalee W. Washington (166)	Rosalee W. Washington

Index

A

Abraham, Paul 46
Adger, Daniel 2, 133
Admore, Simon 43
African Methodist Episcopal Church 12
Agnew, Spiro T. (Vice President) 22
Aiken, Bernice 21, 97
Aiken, Carrie Lou 42-43, 46, 47, 108
Aiken, Clay 20-21, 35, 89, 131, 140
Aiken, Edward 59, 61, 91
Aiken, Lee Esther 68
Aiken, Rochelle 68
Aiken, Samuel 58
Aiken, Samuel Edward 122
Aiken, Sherri 92, 150
Aiken, Stella M. 59, 97, 122
Aiken, Tyrone E. ix, 27, 33, 34, 35, 91, 98, 130, 147, 148, 149, 153, 154, 156, 157, 158, 159
Albright, J. W. 16, 17, 35, 136, 137
Albright, T.A. 64
Alston, Anthony 74
Anderson, Helen ix, 83
Anderson, R. 38
Ashe, Gracie 41
Avery Institute (Charleston, S.C.) 41, 109, 112
Ayers, E. R. 116

B

Bacote, Naomi ix, 112
Bailey, Dorothy 31, 32, 34, 83, 97, 151, 153, 156, 158
Ball, S. (Rev.) 55
Balm in Gilead 117-118
Barlowe, Emmet 152
Barron, Daniel Benjamin 18, 55, 57, 64, 65, 66, 67, 99, 137
Barron, Wilhemenia Alston vii, 43, 46, 55, 58, 64, 66, 67, 96, 97, 99, 99, 100, 108
Baylock, Alfred 27, 147
Baylock, John 131
Beard, J.E. (Dr.) 57
Bell, Barbara 157
Bell, Charles 22, 28, 31, 82, 85, 140, 141, 142, 147, 148, 149
Bell, Josh 24, 89, 144
Bell, Lillie 104
Bellamy, Elijah 64
Bellamy, Elis J. 134
Bellamy, Samuel W. 134, 135
Bennett, Earnestine 43, 72
Bennett, Harold W. 89, 91
Bennett, I.W. (Rev.) 57
Bennett, Mary 129
Bennett, Mary L. 72
Bennett, Nathan 124, 129
Bennett, Sam 20, 22, 71, 72, 82, 85, 129, 139, 140
Bennett, Samuel Jr. 72
Bianchi, B.A. (Rev.) 55
Bible Sojourn Society 28-29, 134, 135
Blake, Ollie 97
Bland, Clyde 91
Boags, Sadie 41
Bolgers, Charles (Rev.) 74
Boone, Margaret 46
Bowens, Reverend 72

Bowman, Mary 71, 72, 96, 97, 111, 138
Bowman, Odessa 97
Boyd, Rick 91
Bozier, Sarah x
Bradley, Eric 85, 98
Brebner, Alec 158
Britton, Leila 46
Broadwater, Thomas 26
Brown, A. 74
Brown, Alethia N. 60, 61
Brown, Alvoronie 43, 64
Brown, Amelia 136
Brown, Barbara 56, 64
Brown, Charles F. 60, 61
Brown, Charles H. (Rev.) 59, 64, 69, 131
Brown, Christine 55
Brown, Earl 56, 64
Brown, Katrina 43
Brown, Larry 34
Brown, Leroy 56, 64
Brown, Lucretia 64
Brown, Roosevelt (Rev.) 32, 34, 55, 56, 64
Brown, S.D. (Rev.) 56
Brown, Susie 71
Brown, Willie 22, 89, 140, 142
Brownville Cemetery 28
Broyhill Industry 141
Bryant, Theodosia 72
Buddin, Mable 44
Buffet, Marc 2, 3, 53, 54, 133
Buggs, Charles T. 30-33, 35, 82, 94, 148, 149, 150, 151, 152, 153
Buggs, Victoria 32
Bull, Elias 145
Bunkum, Gail ix
Burt, Albert 131
Burton, Lucy 135, 136

C

Cain, Laura H. 8
Cain, Richard Harvey (Rev.) vii, 1, 2, 6, 39, 66, 135
Cakely, James 85
Campbell, Bernesta 97
Campbell, Clarence 89, 91
Campbell, Susan 134
Carn, Jamie 92
Carpenter, Andrew 31, 130, 150
Carpenter, Ryan 68
Carpenter, Sarah 74, 97
Carpenter, W. E. 74
Carroll, I.D. 43, 64
Carroll, Mildred 43, 56, 64, 67
Carroll, Sam 43, 64
Carter, Jimmy (Pres.) 23
Causey, Al 136
Causey, R.G. (Sheriff) 137
Centenary Methodist Episcopal Church 70
Charleston News and Courier 13
Chavis, P. J. 54
Cheverie, Robert 34, 155
Chinners, George 138
Civic League vii, 21, 30, 32, 93-98, 142, 149, 150, 153, 154, 155, 157, 165. See also Cosmopolitan Civic League
Clinton, William Jefferson (Pres.) 151
Clyde, Patrick 91
Cobin, Ethel 59
Cochran, Rufus (Rev.) 58, 69
Cole, Anita 112
Colt, E. H. 54
Connors, John 32, 150
Constantine, Elliot 158
Cook, Herbert 22, 140
Cooper, Marthena E. 11
Cooper, Russ 24, 85, 88
Coppin, L. H. 66

Corbin, George (Rev.) 58, 59
Cordes, Hayward (Rev.) ix
Cosmopolitan Civic League 19, 93, 138. See also Civic League
Cotton, Anna Elizabeth 11
Cox, Mildred S. (Rev.) 89, 97, 141
Cox, Samuel Richard 20, 23, 26, 27, 89, 91, 130, 131
Craig, Florence 96, 97
Craven, Jay 92
Craven, Kenny 92
Craven, Michael 92
Craven, Norman 26, 27, 144, 145
Crocker, Mike 92
Crosby, Officer 85
Crum, William D. 116
Cummings, J. P. (Rev.) 61, 67, 69
Curry, Dan (Rev.) 57
Cuttino, Daisy 43
Cuttino, Franklin 43
Cuttino, Joseph 43
Cuttino, William 43

Daniel, L. A. 89
Daniels, Edward 43, 131
Daniels, Elouise 71
Daniels, Herbert 43, 131
Daniels, Jean 43
Daniels, Leroy 27, 43, 91, 130, 145, 146, 147, 152
Daniels, Lillie Mae 72
Daniels, Mildred 43, 72
Daniels, Nathan 71
Deas, Virgil 156, 158
Dease, Barbara 32, 34, 97, 152, 153, 156
Dennison, Rebecca 134
Dennison, Thomas S. 134
Devine, Ernestine 31, 159
Deweese, Charles 43, 48
Deweese, Sarah 34, 155

Dezelle, Adonis 73, 74, 134
Dezelle, Adonis Jr. 43
Dezelle, Della 74
Dezelle, Gloria 107
Dezelle, Henry 74, 124
Dezelle, Marie 74, 124
Dezelle, Phyliss 74
Dezelle, Sarah 43, 49
Dickerson, Enoch 29, 83, 148, 149, 152, 156
Dickerson, Henrietta 135
Dickerson, Zanitha M. 150
Douglas, Annette 28, 29, 97, 148
Douglas, Elaine 97
Douglas, Elizabeth 72
Douglas, Harold 23, 26, 43, 89, 92, 142, 144
Douglas, Hillary 148
Douglas, Janie 96, 97, 129
Douglas, John 88, 89, 91, 129, 131
Douglas, John Jr. 43
Douglas, John J. 89
Douglas, Kirby 125, 129
Douglas, Luther 125, 129
Doyle, Earl 43, 49, 56, 64
Drayton, Richard 20, 22, 88, 89, 92
Duberry, Charles 27, 31, 32, 34, 84, 89, 92, 131, 145, 147, 148, 149, 150, 151, 153, 156
Duberry, Eloise 97
Duberry, Franklin 131
Duberry, Levi 24, 26, 143, 144
Duberry, Lorraine 97
Duffy, George 54
Dunmeyer Hill, S.C. 73
Dunmeyer, Ann 134, 135
Dunmeyer, Joseph 73
Dunn, Frank vii, ix, 130, 157, 163
Dutton, Clarence Edward (Capt.) 37
Dyson, Myra W. 166

E

Earthquake (1886) 37, 134
Ebenezer A.M.E. Church Red Club 56
Ebenezer A.M.E. Church Senior Choir 59
Ebenezer A.M.E. Church Sunday School vii, 53, 53, 63-69, 98
Ebenezer African Methodist Episcopal Church vii, 2, 33, 53-62, 133, 138, 139, 155, 156
Eden, Marie S. 29, 134
Eden, William 53, 63, 133
Edwards, Anna 71, 72, 96, 97
Edwards, Catherine (Kate) 56, 59, 64
Edwards, Edmund 19, 71, 72
Edwards, Edna 71
Edwards, Edward 19
Edwards, Ned I. (Rev.) 58, 68, 69
Enoch, Reverend 55
Everett, Earnest E. 112

F

Farmer, L. L. (Rev.) 55
Faulks, A. M. (Rev.) 74
Felder family 79
Felder, Isabel 78
Fennick, John 17, 35, 135
Fiddie, D. 89, 92
Fielding, Bernard R. ix, 24, 89
Fielding, Mark 30
Fielding, Timothy 30
Fielding, Zelma R. 26, 27, 28, 29, 30, 32, 35, 95, 144, 145, 147, 148, 149
Fields, Geraldine 46
Ford, Becky 152
Forrest, Ella 41, 112
Forrest, G. 41
Fraser, Harriett 134
Frasier, Samuel 19
Frasier, William 70
Frazier, Dianna 134
Frazier, Hattie 66, 67, 96, 97
Frazier, Officer 85
Frazier, Samuel 58
Friendship Inspirational Church of God in Christ vii, 78-79
Frieson, B. 44

G

Gadsden, Frank 112
Gadsden, James S. (Rev.) 72
Gadsden, Josh (Rev.) 58, 68
Gale, Johnnie 43
Gantt, Charles 91, 98, 153
Gardner, George 19, 82, 85, 139
Gardner, Mary 56, 57, 82, 125
Generette, Reverend 72
German, Elnora 124
German, Michael Lewis ix, 124
Gibbs, James 135
Gibbs, John 70
Gleaton, Anna Ruth Williams (Rev.) ix, 32, 34, 59, 61, 98, 154, 157, 159
Gleaton, Charles 89, 92
Gleaton, Denise RaeShawn 95, 149
Gleaton, Michelle 95, 147
Glover, Curtis 20
Glover, Dorothy ix, 59, 97, 141
Glover, Edna Elaine 67, 68, 143
Glover, Gail 68
Glover, Sherman 130
Glover, Sonia 10, 31, 32, 149, 150, 155, 157, 159
Glover, Vermel B. 24, 142
Godfrey, John 17, 35
Goldman, Mary H. 57
Goode, Constance 43
Goode, Emily 71
Goode, Harold 43, 49

Goode, Hazel 43
Goode, Lloyd A. 89, 92
Goode, Maria 43
Goodwin, Annette Douglas 27, 147, 148
Gordon, Floyd 74
Graham, E. W. (Rev.) 56, 66
Grant, Adrama 63
Grant, Edmond 64
Grant, Hector 2, 18, 63, 133, 137
Grant, Jessie 135
Grant, Joseph 55, 63
Grant, Naomi 44
Gravely, Blanche 44
Gray, B.N. (Rev.) 58
Green, Katie 63
Greene, Alfonzo 30, 31, 149, 150, 151, 152, 153
Greene, Rochelle A. ix, 122-123
Greer, Sylvia 57
Gregg, Elias J. (Rev.) 54
Grooms, Linda 31, 149, 153
Guthke, Wilmot 88

H

Hamilton, Leola 134
Hammond, Susan 55, 134, 136
Hammond, W. F. 15-16, 18, 35, 135, 136, 137
Hampton, Christine W. i, iii, xi, 62, 97, 143, 152, 153, 165-166
Hampton, Jade 68, 165
Hampton, James Charles v, ix, x, 28, 31, 34, 69, 83, 84, 89, 91, 94, 125, 126 -128, 147, 149, 150, 151, 152, 153, 154, 156, 157, 158, 165
Hampton, James Christopher vii, 101-102, 165
Hampton, Tanya Michelle 165
Hardee, Betty Seabrook 24, 144

Hardee, Freddie 43, 48
Hardee, Nathaniel P. 85, 141
Hardee, Nellie 135
Hardee, Richard 43
Harris, Eliza K. 137
Harrison, David 131
Harrison, Isaac 131
Harrison, Joseph 132
Harrison, Wilbur 43
Hawkins, Falcon 155, 156
Haynes, Kevin 92
Haynes, Tonya 98
Henderson, P. C. (Rev.) 44
Hendricks, John 91
Henry, Wardean Nichols 13
Hicks, Michael 91, 92
Hill, Clyde 43, 56, 64
Hill, David R. 28, 41, 63, 66, 103, 134, 135
Hill, David Seabrook vii, 93, 103
Hill, Edith 43
Hill, Elizabeth 60, 69
Hill, Gordon 43, 60
Hill, Gordon Jr. 92
Hill, John 134
Hill, Louise ix, 93, 97, 103, 138
Hill, Mattie Seabrook 41, 136, 137
Hill, Richard 83, 85, 91, 156
Hines, David Sr. 54
Hofen, Karl 92
Hoffius, Stephen x
Hoffman, F. W. 116
Holloway, Samuel 136
Holman, Alonzo F. 104
Holman, Alonzo William (Rev.) vii, ix, 10, 21, 43, 56, 61, 62, 64, 104
Holman, Eliza K. 134
Holman, E.K. 3, 14
Holman, Gerald ix, 64
Holman, Lillie Bell Ross 21, 104
Holman, Mary 56, 64
Holman, Robert M. 137

Holman, Ross 104
Holman, Timothy 21, 43, 64
Holmes, Leola P. 24, 144
Horlback, Olivia x
Howard, Carolyn A. ix
Howard, Gloria Noisette 13
Howard, Officer 85
Howell, Mary 32, 153
Huger, Harold 92
Huger, Lorraine 92
Hunt, Grace 46
Hurricane Hugo (1989) 29, 147-148, 149

I

Iricks, Laura 97
Irvin, Tom 91

J

Jackson, Annette 44
Jackson, F.C. 44
Jackson, L. T. (Rev.) 72
Jackson, Sheri Aiken 131
Jacobs, Albertha 96, 97, 128
Jacobs, C. F. (Rev.) 70
Jacobs, Dwayne 125, 130
Jacobs, George ix, 20, 22, 23, 26, 27, 88, 89, 92, 125, 128, 132, 140, 142, 144, 145, 148
Jacobs, Martina 32, 152, 153
Jacobs, Samuel 29, 148
James, Azalee 107
James, Bobby 43
James, Christine 43
James, Eleanor Franklin 108
James, Lawrence (Dr.) vii, 107-108
James, Leroy 107
James, Louis 107
James, Robert 107
Jenkins, A. 134
Jenkins, Daniel J. 116

Jenkins, Esau 45
Jennings, Cherise 123-124
Jennings, Ernest 31, 34, 94, 95, 123, 132, 150, 151, 153, 154
Jennings, H. J. (Bishop) 76
Jennings, J.J. Jr. (Bishop) ix
Jennings, Jessie 76, 78
Jennings, Jessie Jr. 78
Jennings, Willa Mae 123
Jervay, W. R. (Rev.) 72
Johnson, Edward L. 79
Johnson, Elise 97
Johnson, Isaac (Rev.) 60, 69
Johnson, Johnnie J. 79
Johnson, Johnny 132
Johnson, Lady Bird 140
Johnson, Norma Lee 112
Johnson, W. H. 116
Jones, E.T. (Rev.) 69
Jones, Sara Bell 74
Jordan, Donavan 34

K

Keller, George 136
Keller, James 134
Keller, Louise 43
Keller, Mammie 71
Keller, Mary Ellen 43
Keller, Ruth 71
Keller, Samuel 19, 71, 72, 88, 138
Keller, Thelma 43, 49
Kelly, Georgia 69, 97
Kelly, Marshall 34, 92, 154
Kennedy, Katie N. 11
Kitt, Mary M. 55, 64, 66

L

Ladson, C. E. 16
Ladson, Reverend 55
Lary, Sandra 28, 147
Latten, Alma ix, 112

Lavally, Pompey G. 17, 35
Lavally, Rosalee 35
Lee, P. C. (Rev.) 55
Lee, Samuel J. 3
Leland, Harris 11
Lenear, Mrs. 55
Levy, John 113
Lewis, Marthena 11
Lincoln Village (early name for Lincolnville) 2
Lincoln, Abraham vii, 3
Lincoln, Gladys 32, 97
Lincolnville Elementary School vii, 14, 16, 23, 33, 34, 39-51, 99, 104, 107, 109, 117, 121, 122, 124, 125, 126, 129, 138, 139, 141, 142, 145, 165, 166. See also Williams Graded School
Lincolnville Emancipation Association 135
Lincolnville jail 82, 152
Lincolnville Police Department vii, 81-85, 158
Lincolnville Volunteer Fire Department vii, 26, 87, 92, 153, 155, 156
Lincolnville, S.C.; founding of, 1-3
Lindsey, L. H. 112
Linen, Bessie 59, 60, 97
Linen, Ralph 60, 132
Livingston, J. V. (Rev.) 72
Locklear, Carla 150
Locklear, Leverne 34, 154
Loggan, Margaret 59
Lowry, Robert 66
Lucas, Reverend 55
Lucka, Melinda 159
Lucky, Crystal (Dr.) ix
Lydia Baptist Church vii, 80

M

Mack, Leon 43
Mack, Mary 43, 71, 72
Mack, Mozelle 72
Mack, Oliver 43
Mack, Susan 134
Major, Cruel 134
Mance, A. Williams 14
Mance, Barbara 43
Mance, C. W. (Rev.) 55
Mance, Earnestine 96, 97
Mance, Emmaline A. 14, 41, 55, 64, 66, 67, 68
Mance, George Clayton ix, 14, 20, 35, 140
Mance, Mildred 14
Mance, P.J. 14
Mance, William 14, 43
Manley, Calvin 43, 49
Manley, Eunice 43
Manley, Joseph (Marshal) 81, 85, 138
Martin, Grace 41
Martin, Mary 74
Martin, Milkman 138
Maryville, S.C. 1
Mayes, Nellie 46
McCown, R. M. 137
McCray, John Henry 109-110
McCray, Rachel 57, 64, 66, 67, 68, 96, 97, 109, 110
McDonald, Allen 155
McDowell, Blair 91, 92
McKinley, Jeremiah (Rev.) 59, 60, 69
McQueen, C.W. (Rev.) 55, 64
Meyers, Leroy 85
Mickens, Henry 3, 135
Middleton, Eliza 136
Middleton, Jessie (Rev.) 56
Miller, J. H. 89, 92
Miller, Leon 88, 91, 138 140

Miller, Peter 70
Miller's Grocery Store 138
Milligan, Judge 134
Mincey, Mr. 92
Mingo, Reverend 72
Mitchell, Julia 41
Mitchell, Pamela 132
Montgomery, William M. Jr. 24, 89, 92, 144
Mood, Benjamin 94
Mood, Thomas 94
Morris Brown A.M.E. Church 2, 10
Morris, Charles 157
Morris, Calvin (Rev.) 59, 69
Moses, Christine 107
Mount Zion Baptist Church vii, 73-75
Muldrew, Anna 71
Muldrew, Margaret 43
Muldrew, Mildred 43, 48
Muldrew, Thelma 43
Muldrew, William 43, 71
Myers, Leroy 24
Myers, Ruth M. 112

Nazareth Holiness Church of Deliverance #2 vii, 76-77
Nelson, Emily Manley x
Nero, Reverend 56
Nesbitt, R.W. 15
Nesbitt, Richard 136
Newman, Ernest (Rev.) 72
Nichols, Benjamin S. 11
Nichols, Decatur Ward (Rev.) 13
Nichols, Henry M. 11
Nichols, Hicksey 11
Nichols, Laverne 155
Nichols, Lewis Ruffin (Rev.) 2, 11-13, 35, 38, 54, 133
Nichols, Louisa 11

Nichols, Nancy Eunice 11
Nichols, Robert 11
Nichols, Robert III 11
Nichols, Robert Jr. 11
Nichols, Samuel W. 11
Nichols, Stephan 11
Nichols, William E. 11
Nixon, Richard (Pres.) 23
Noble, Fred 20, 34, 68, 69, 88, 131
Noble, Fred III 69
Noble, Juanita 69
Noble, Lucille R. x, 59, 68, 69, 97, 141
Noisette, Beatrice 11
Noisette, Bettye Joe 13
Noisette, Helen B. 13
Noisette, Lewis Ruffin x, 34
Noisette, Lurline M. 13
North Lincolnville, S.C. 135

"Oh Lincolnville," by Frank Dunn 157, 163
O'Neil, Anthony 27, 145
O'Neil, George 134
Owens, Susan 8, 14, 39, 40, 134

P

Pasley, James 85
Patrick, F. 41
Pavlovich, Leo 26, 85, 144
Pedalino, Joe 91, 92
Perry, Fanny 41
Perry, John P. 135
Peterson, Samuel F. 3
Peterson, William 135
Philadelphia Baptist Church (Ladson, S.C.) 74
Pinckney, Thomas 135
Platt, Officer 85
Polk, Helene Seele x, 17, 132

Pon Pon (early name for Lincolnville) 2
Powers, Bernard (Dr.) x
Presley, Clark 91, 92
Pressley, Gerri 155
Price, Josephine M. 134
Prioleau, Rosalee 17
Promised Land, S.C. 1
Pump Pond (early name for Lincolnville) 1, 2
Pump Pond Swamp (early name for Lincolnville) 1
Pump Swamp (early name for Lincolnville) 1
Pyatt, M. P. (Rev.) 72

Queeman, Pamela 159
Quincy, Dr. 98

Ransom, Reverend 54
Ready, Richard A. vii, 18, 64, 111-112, 135
Reagan, Ronald (Pres.) 23, 146
Reid, Maude K. 13
Rhames, Reverend 55
Rhodes, Cathy 156
Richardson, Betty 139
Richardson, Samuel 139
Riley, Charlotte S. vii, x, 113, 134
Riley, Cornelius 113
Riley, Richard (Gov.) 106
Roberson, Robert 91
Roberts, Albert 92
Roberts, D. K. 92
Roberts, F.A. (Rev.) 22, 24, 140, 142, 144
Roberts, Ruth 154
Roberts, Steven 91, 92
Roberts-Shepherd, Ruth 34

Robinson, Bobby 91, 92
Robinson, Ida 137
Robinson, Isaac 2
Roosevelt, Theodore (Pres.) 115
Rosenwald, Julius 111
Rosenwald School 44, 111. See also Lincolnville Elementary School.
Ross, Charles P. 21-28, 32, 35, 82, 86, 89, 140, 141, 142, 143, 144, 145, 146, 147
Ross, Charles, Municipal Complex 32, 49, 76, 144, 157, 149
Ross, Ida Brown 59, 64, 67, 68, 96, 97
Ross, Miller 88, 125, 128
Ross, Ruth M. 19, 20, 22, 57, 68, 97, 128
Rowe, Janie 71
Rowe, Lucille 43, 72

Saint Luke A.M.E. Church 56
Salley, Alonza 43
Salley, Dorothy 97
Salley, Eddie Sr. (Rev.) 74
Salley, Ernest 132
Salley, Hattie Mae 83, 97
Salley, Leon 43
Salley, Leon (Rev.) x, 74
Salley, Mattie 74, 97
Salley, Michael 132
Salley, Rosalee 43
Salters, M.B. (Rev.) 2, 133
Salters, R. 16
Sanders, Joyce 92
Schneider, Joseph 85
Schutt, Gladys 44
Seabrook, Mattie 40, 41, 63, 115
Seal, J. A. 116

Seele, Charles Augustus 16, 17, 18, 35, 71, 72, 81, 111, 118, 134, 135, 137
Seele, Charles Jr. 17, ju71, 117
Seele, Edna 72, 96, 97
Seele, Helene 71, 72, 132
Seele, Isabelle 16, 18, 71, 72, 96
Seele, Luella Doris 22, 46, 71, 117
Seele, Pernessa C. vii, x, 71, 117
Seele, Susan A. 135
Seele, William Jr. 16, 18, 35
Seele, William Sr. 16, 17, 18, 19, 35, 71, 72, 118, 134
Sellers, Carrie x, 97, 124
Sellers, Eric 92
Sellers, Theodore 32, 92, 89, 124
Shannon, Leland 27, 30, 31, 34, 91, 92, 145, 150, 151, 152, 153, 154, 156, 158
Sharp, David 85
Shivers, Officer 85
Simmons family 79
Simmons, Carolee x, 78
Simmons, Katura 68
Simmons, Lewis H. (Rev.) 74
Simmons, Nicole 68
Simmons, Philip 23, 142
Simpson family 79
Simpson, Edward 91, 92
Singleton, Arthur 132
Singleton, Booker T. 132
Singleton, Ivory 62
Singleton, Jackie 62
Singleton, Lottie 59, 60, 97
Skiba, Ed 91, 92
Skinner, Shirley 68
Skinner, Tommy 28, 147
Smalls, Pearly M. x
Smalls, S.J. 70
Smalls, Sofia 132
Smith, Alice R. Williams 59, 62, 68, 69, 83, 97, 98
Smith, Daniel 135
Smith, Gerald E. 104
Smith, Jesse 13, 35, 53, 137
Smith, Lavonce 43
Snyder, Leo 85
South Carolina Land Commission 8
South Carolina Railway Company 1, 133
Sparks, M. S. 55, 63
Spears, Reverend 72
Spells, Hazel 139
Squire, John 49, 121
Squire, Naomi 57
Steadman, Martha 135
Steele, J. S. 135
Steele, Walter 2, 40, 53, 133
Stevenson, Levern (Rev.) 61
Stevenson, Maxine 61
Stewart, Georgette Mance 20
Stillwell, Officer 85
Strother, William C. (Rev.) 72
Sweet, Reverend 57

Tager, Kay 24, 26, 143, 144
Tarver, Mary Holman 21
Taylor, Paul 76, 78
Taylor, Sioux Nichols 13
Thomas, James 85
Thurmond, J. Strom (Sen.) 22, 82
Tobin, Mary Miles 63
Toomer, Martha A. 112
Towns, Patricia 119
Towns, Stephen vii, x, 119-120
Trammell, Officer 85
Turner, Inez 97
Turner, Leonard 152

Vann, Kenneth (Officer) 82, 84, 85, 153
Venner, Carolyn x

Vesey, Denmark 7
Vesey, Robert 7
Village of Lincoln (early name for Lincolnville) 2

W

Wade, Emmaline 136
Wagoner, J.B. 32, 91, 146, 151
Walden, Thomas 92
Walker, Iris 85
Wallace, Catherine 133
Washington, Arnic J. v, x, 22, 23, 26, 88, 89, 90, 92, 140, 142, 144, 145, 166-167
Washington, Gertrude Sabb 19, 71, 72, 96, 97
Washington, Mose Jerome (Rev.) 18, 35, 66, 68
Washington, Myra 94, 143
Washington, Raymond I. 94, 131, 166
Washington, Rosalee Williams i, iii, xi, 10, 24, 26, 30, 32, 34, 46, 62, 67, 68, 95, 97, 141, 142, 150, 151, 152, 153, 154, 166, 167
Washington, William H. 15, 35, 64, 111, 115, 116
Watson, Doris 46
Weaver, Dennis 92
Weaver, Joe 26, 27, 144, 145
Weidman, Jean 32, 150, 153
Wesley Christian Church 72
Wesley Methodist Episcopal Church vii, 16, 17, 65, 70-72, 138
Wesley United Methodist Episcopal Church. See Wesley Methodist Episcopal Church
White, Donnie 28, 85, 146, 147
White, Eliza 135
White, George 20, 85, 139
White, Mary 34

Wigfall, Mildred Mance x, 122
Wigfall, S. 44
Wilkes, John (Mrs.) 113
Wilkins, Mattie 44
Williams family 79
Williams Graded School 14, 19, 39, 40, 41, 103, 135, 139, 141, 145. See also Lincolnville Elementary School
Williams, A. Tony 2, 14, 15, 20, 35, 39, 40, 41, 134, 135
Williams, Alice 43, 49, 57, 67
Williams, Anna Rebeca (Rev.) x, 96, 97, 166
Williams, Anna Ruth 68
Williams, Annabelle 97
Williams, Bo 91, 92
Williams, Catherine 133
Williams, Christine 64
Williams, Christopher Elijah v, 19, 57, 60, 61, 125
Williams, Clarence 43, 49, 131
Williams, Clayton x, 64, 121-122
Williams, Della W. 11
Williams, Essie Mae 43
Williams, Gamerlear 79, 89, 91, 142
Williams, Geraldine D. x
Williams, Gloria 132
Williams, Herbert 43, 49, 56, 64
Williams, James Allen 47, 125, 126
Williams, Jessie x, 125
Williams, Laverne 30, 31, 34, 83, 97, 148, 149, 152, 153, 154
Williams, Mary 27, 32, 97, 147, 151
Williams, Robbie 94
Williams, Roosevelt 43
Williams, Rosalee W. 43, 48, 56, 57, 64
Williams, Sam 31, 92, 149
Williams, Sandy M. 94, 95, 125-126

Williams, Willie 43, 132
Williamson, Marie S. 135
Willis, Eugene 46, 141
Wilson, B. C. M. (Rev.) 72
Wilson, Etta 44
Wilson, J. T. (John Thomas) 44
Wilson, James 43
Wilson, Marshal 81, 85
Wilson, W. K. 55
Woods, Robert 24, 143
Woodson, Carter G. x, 10
Woodward, Sidney 65
Wooten, E.P. 42-43, 44
Wright, Gwendolyn x

Y

Young, C. I. 44
Young, Jack 134

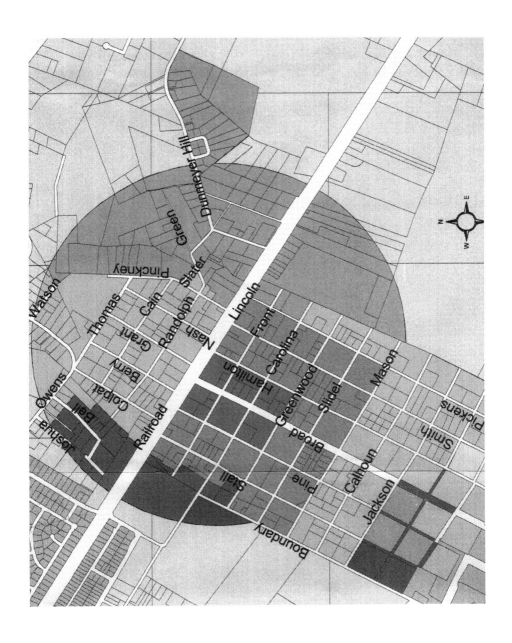

Made in the USA
Lexington, KY
30 January 2014